BEAU COOK'S FOOD PORN

The cookbook that brings together our favourite preoccupations:

FOOD AND SEX.

Lets start with the hors d'oeuvres:
Take equal portions of great ingredients and beautiful bodies.
Stir well. Leave for an hour or so to soak.
Knock discreetly before entering the kitchen.

ENJOY...

WWW.BEAUCOOKSFOODPORN.COM

BEAU COOK'S FOOD PORN

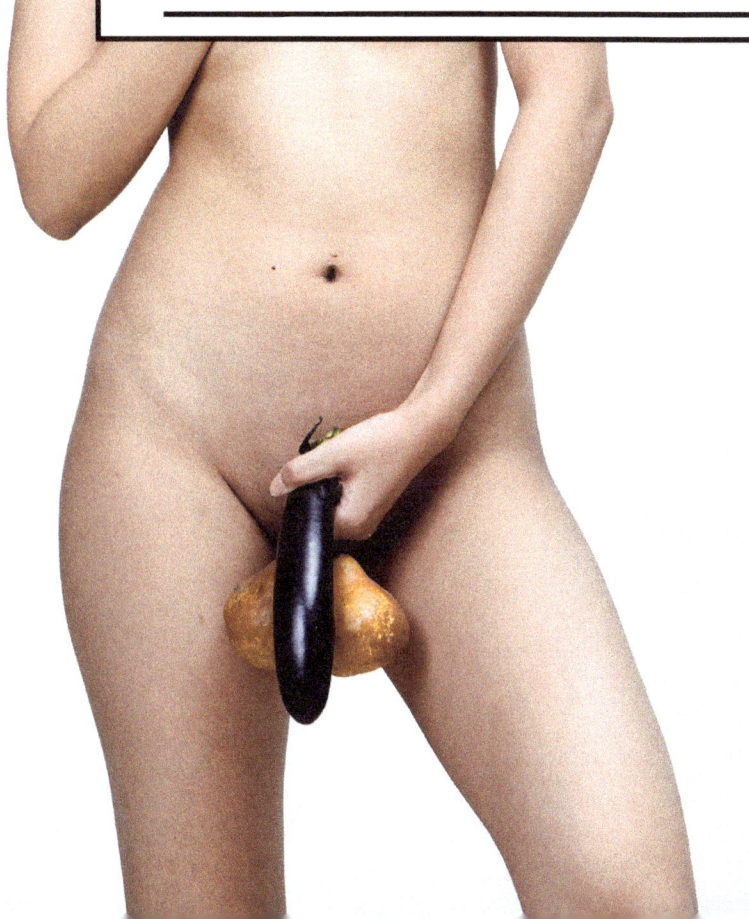

THE FOOD PORN
COOKBOOK

CONTENTS

BEAU COOK **7**

FOREWORD **9**

BREAKFAST IN BED *BLT salad* **13**

WILD OATS *Toasted muesli* **15**

HOT CHOCOLATE *Vegan peanut butter hot chocolate* **17**

JIZZ IMPROVER *Grilled pineapple salad* **19**

FLICKING THE BEAN *Baked bean jaffles* **21**

MORNING GLORY *Guacamole toast with chorizo crumb* **25**

BIG BANANA *Banana pikelets* **27**

CHEESEY PICK UP *Cheesy toast with mushrooms* **29**

GET YOUR FREEK ON *Poached eggs with freekeh, greens and dukkah* **31**

HUMMUSEXUAL *Hummus with smoky harissa* **33**

APHRODISIAC *Natural oysters with shallot dressing* **37**

PRAWN STARS *Chilli and garlic prawns* **39**

STICK IT TO ME *Chicken satay skewers with cucumber salad* **41**

IN THE RAW *Ceviche* **43**

PORK ME *Pork spare ribs with apple and fennel slaw* **45**

STICKY FINGERS *Honey chilli chicken wings* **47**

C-CUPS *Chicken san choi bau* **51**

VEGINA *Vegan bolognaise with zucchini pasta* **53**

THE HAND JOB *Handmade pasta with cherry tomato sauce* **55**

CONTENTS

MEATY ROCKET *Tagliata* **57**

LONG FAT ONES *Hand-cut wedges with spicy tomato relish* **59**

HAVING A PULL *Thai pulled chicken salad* **61**

LICK THE TACO *Vegetarian tacos* **63**

YOU KNEAD IT *Homemade pizza* **67**

JUICY BREASTS *Chicken parmigiana* **69**

SHOULDER RUB *Slow-roasted lamb shoulder with tzatziki* **71**

SHAVED *Grilled zucchini and freekeh salad* **73**

SPICY ROOT *Cajun spiced roast vegetable salad* **75**

GET YOUR BROC OUT *Charred broccoli salad* **77**

MAKE ME SWEAT *Spicy beef cheek curry* **81**

CREAMY MOUTHFUL *Potato & fennel gratin* **83**

BIG BONE *Slow-cooked beef ribs* **85**

STUFF IT IN *Indian baked snapper* **87**

MONEY SHOT *Semifreddo* **91**

BUTTER ME UP *Bread and butter pudding* **93**

BIG TART *Lemon tart* **95**

MAKE ME CRUMBLE *Apple crumble* **97**

GETTING SAUCY *Self-saucing chocolate pudding* **99**

SEXUAL CHOCOLATE *Salted caramel chocolate brownies* **101**

ACKNOWLEDGEMENTS **103**

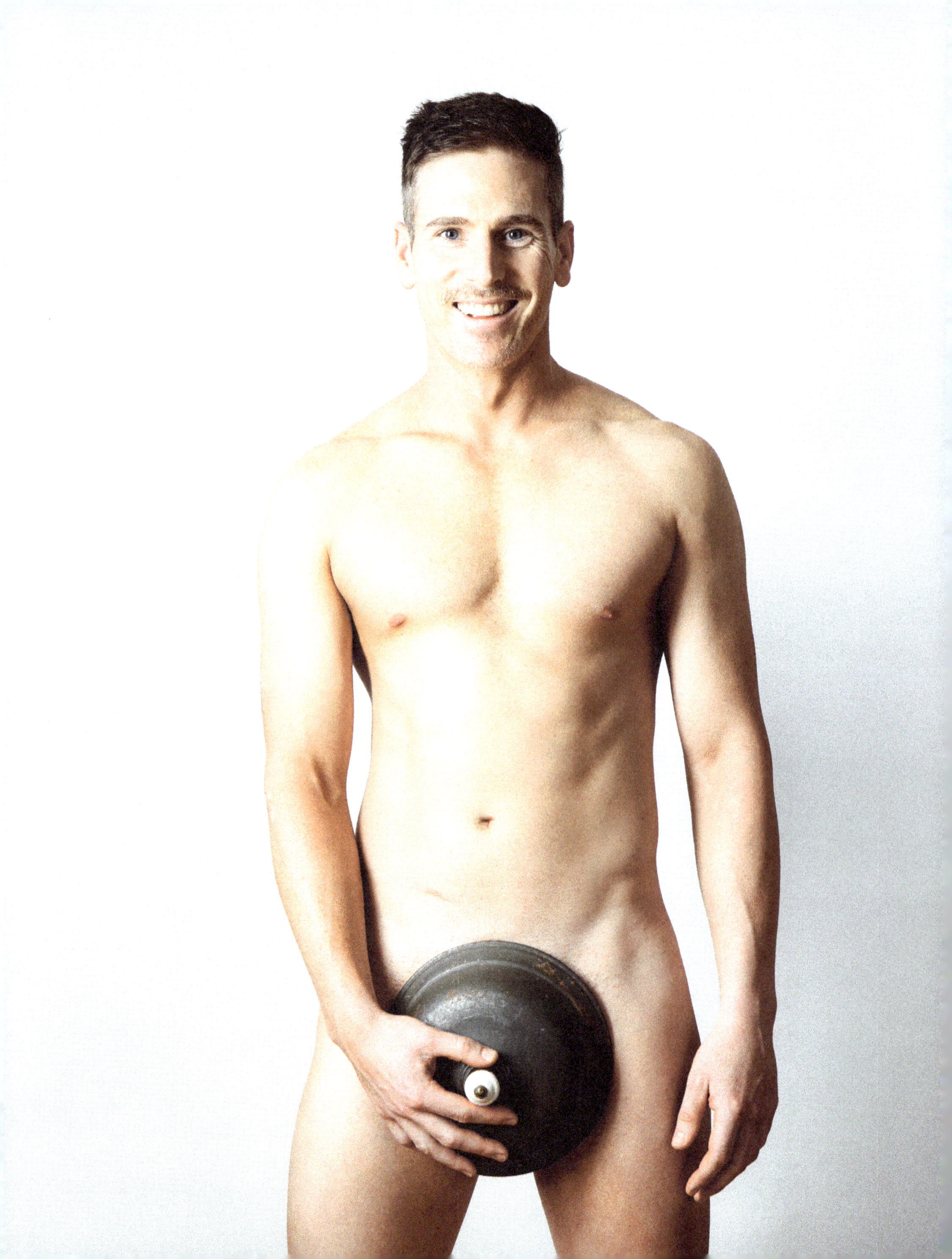

BEAU COOK
BY DAVID WATSON

Brought up from infancy in the Chewton Bushlands of central Victoria, Beau first caught the public's attention as a contestant on Masterchef Australia.

Stir, mix, blend, cut, slice, peel, mash, smash (only avocado), bake, roast, grill, fry, boil, steam, barbeque – you name it Beau has done it with the best. He brought a touch of humour to the otherwise portentous going's-on that is the hallmark of "reality" TV. With twinkling eye and deftness of tongue he saw humour where others could only sense ignominy and disaster. He nursed bruised egos, encouraged the despondent, and helped the hopeless. Beau was never going to become a master chef but he soon became the darling of the TV audience.

Never one to make too much of a fuss about himself Beau ignored the possibility of fame and fortune and is now a full-time professional Fire fighter. He is at heart a team player, best working with – and cooking for – mates.

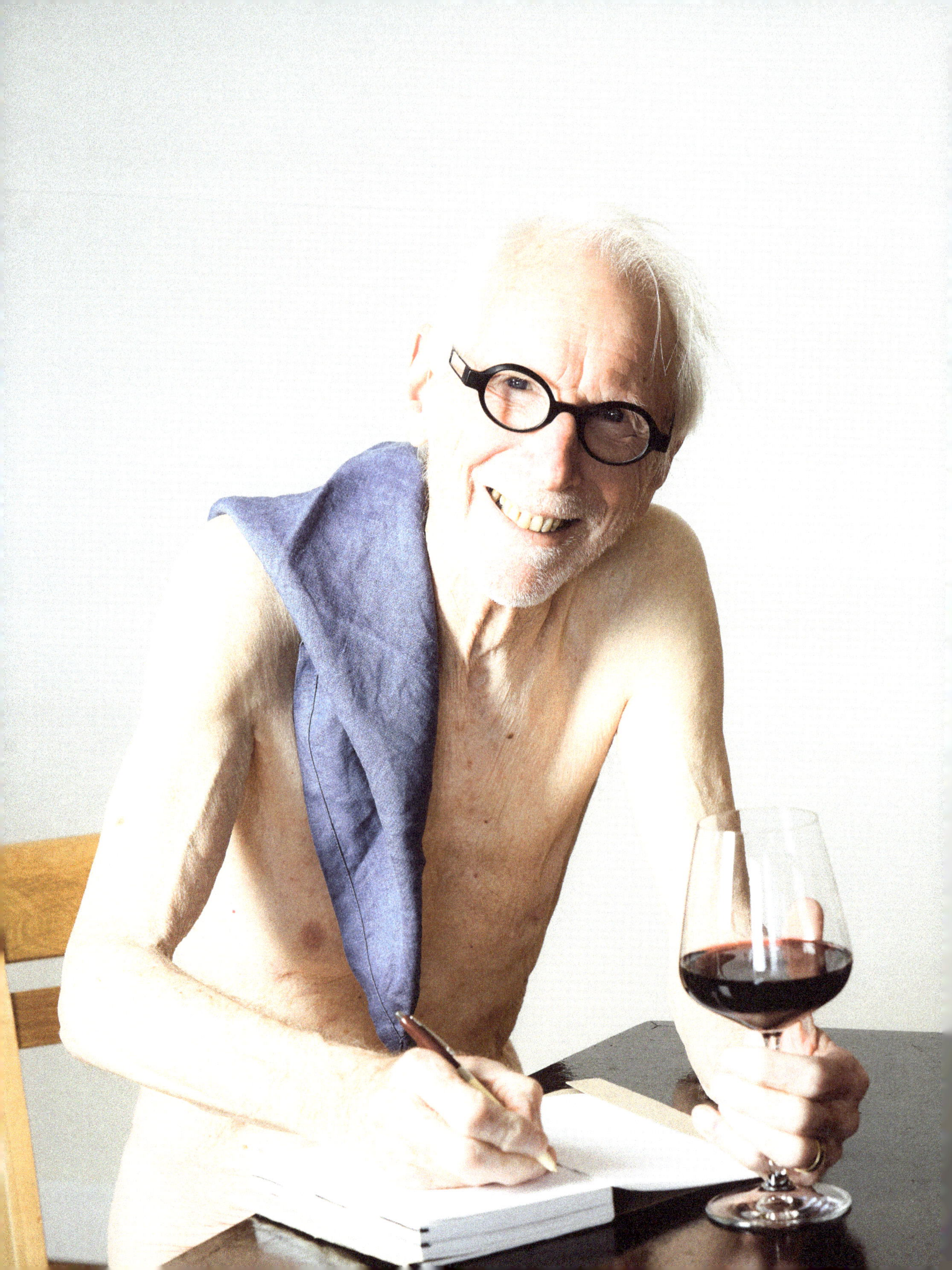

FOREWORD

BY DAVID WATSON

It all started during dinner at a popular Chinese Restaurant. We were celebrating… something. Being alive probably. After a couple of dishes of chicken and sweetporn soup – sorry that should read sweet corn – we were beginning to feel stir crazy. Well, crazy anyway.

I can't remember who mentioned Peking Duck but with a strange gleam in his eye Beau announced he would do something with his TV cooking show experience. He would do what the other competitors did. Write a cookbook! A cookbook with a bit of a twist. Rude Food! That's where the future lies. It's amazing what you can do with a banana, a couple of blood plums and a carefully placed dollop of cream. As for figs… Well, the word itself conjures up nights of bliss for many a randy Italian. And salami… the mind boggles. Well, mine does. Yours might just sit there and quietly sizzle. Beau's emphasis is definitely on the peeking bit. Within these pages you will see pictures of people indulging in play (well two-play and possibly even four-play) and enjoying the delights of good wholesome se… I mean food.

Nobody ever said to him: "Beau stop playing with your food". He has turned what could have been a nasty habit into delightful erotic entertainment. We hope you will enjoy the journey – a romp of rump? – as

Beau Cook's Food Porn.

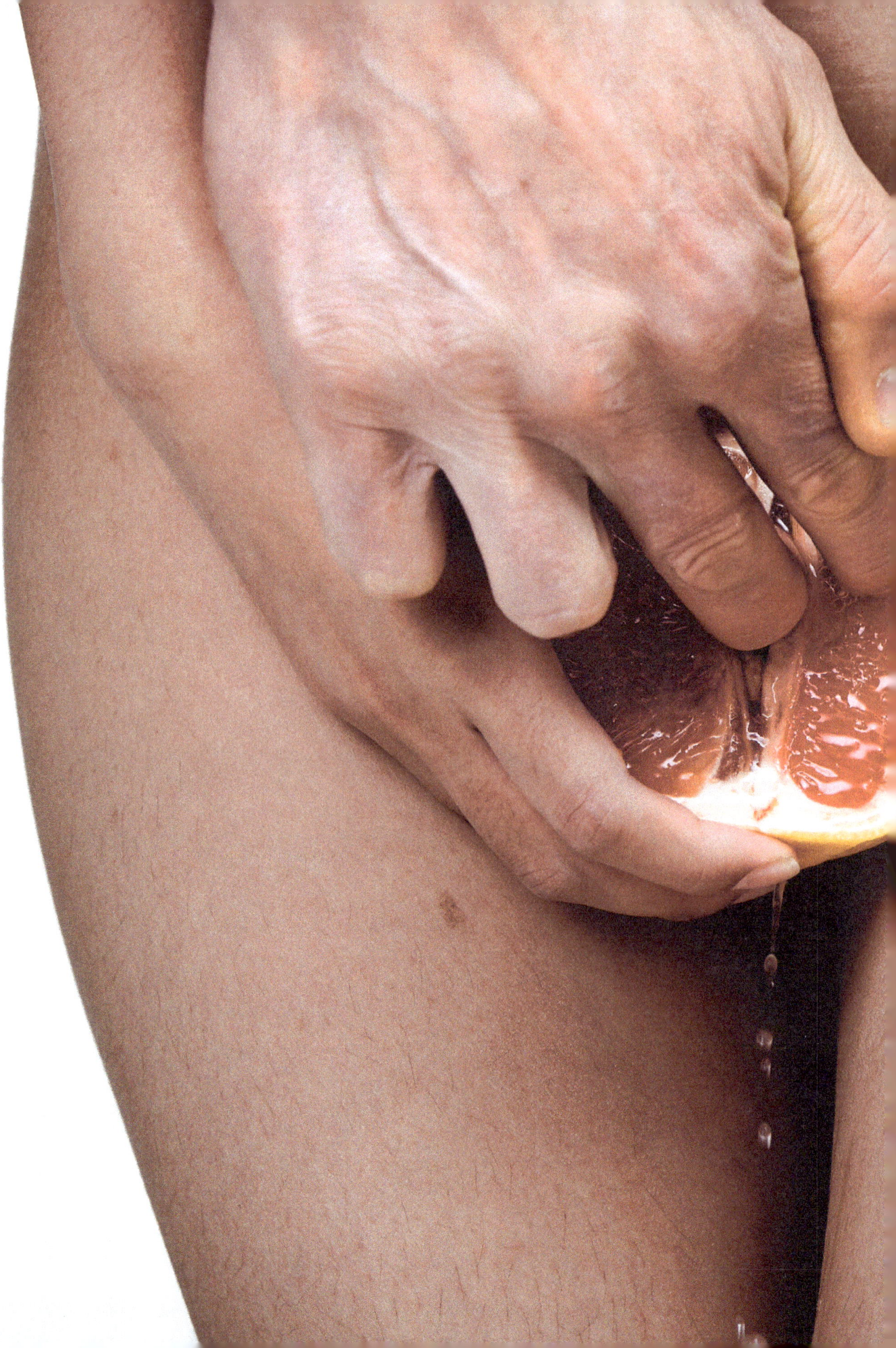

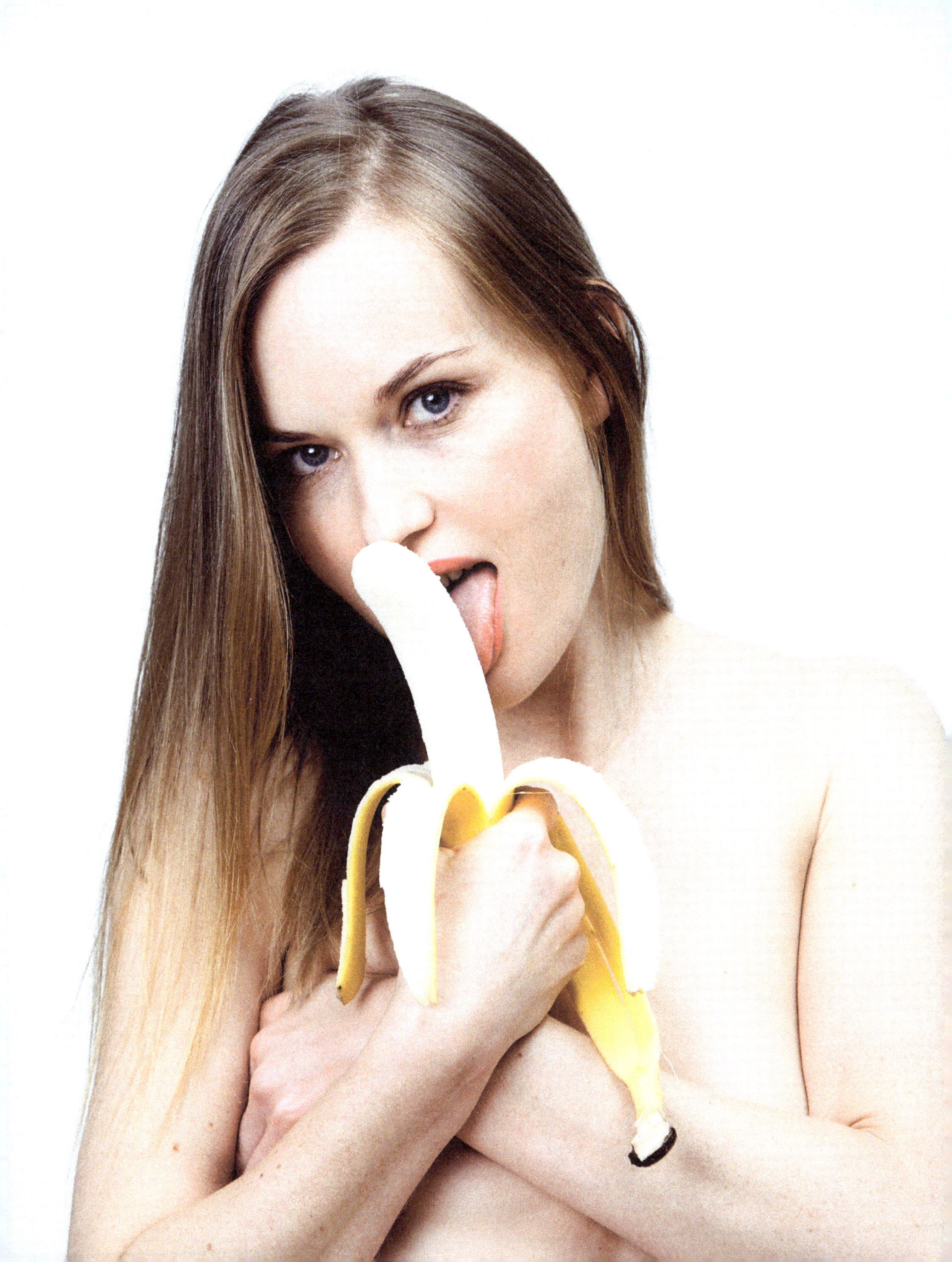

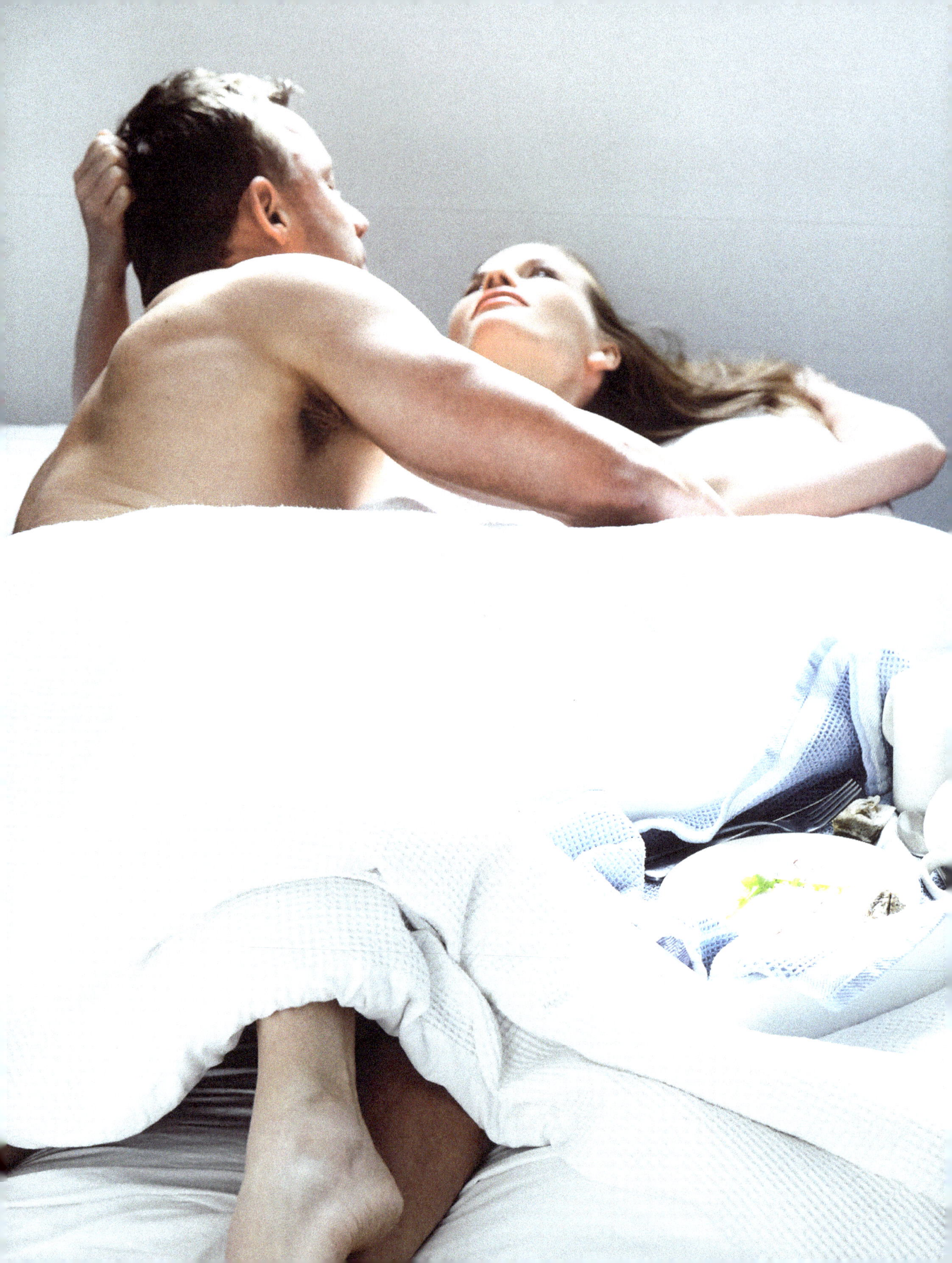

BREAKFAST IN BED

BLT SALAD

A sexy breakfast dish best enjoyed in bed on a lazy Sunday.

SERVES 2

2 extra-large free-range eggs
2 tsp olive oil
4 slices pancetta
2 slices sourdough, cut into soldiers
3 tbs olive oil
1 tbs balsamic vinegar
2 handfuls mixed salad leaves
8 cherry tomatoes, halved
60g buffalo mozzarella, torn into bite-size chunks

1. Bring a small pot of water to the boil. Place eggs into boiling water and cook for 6 minutes. Remove from heat, drain, and place eggs in a bowl of cold water for 2 minutes to cool. Peel eggs and set aside.

2. Meanwhile, heat 2 tsp oil in a frying pan over medium-high heat, add pancetta and cook for 1-2 minutes each side or until crisp. Remove from pan, reserving pan and oil, and drain pancetta on absorbent paper. Tear into quarters.

3. Heat reserved pan over medium-high heat, add sourdough soldiers and cook on all sides until golden brown.

4. Place 3 tbs oil and vinegar in a small bowl and whisk to combine. Season with a pinch of salt and pepper.

5. To serve, layer salad leaves, tomato, mozzarella and pancetta on a plate and drizzle with dressing. Halve each egg and place on top. Serve soldiers on the side.

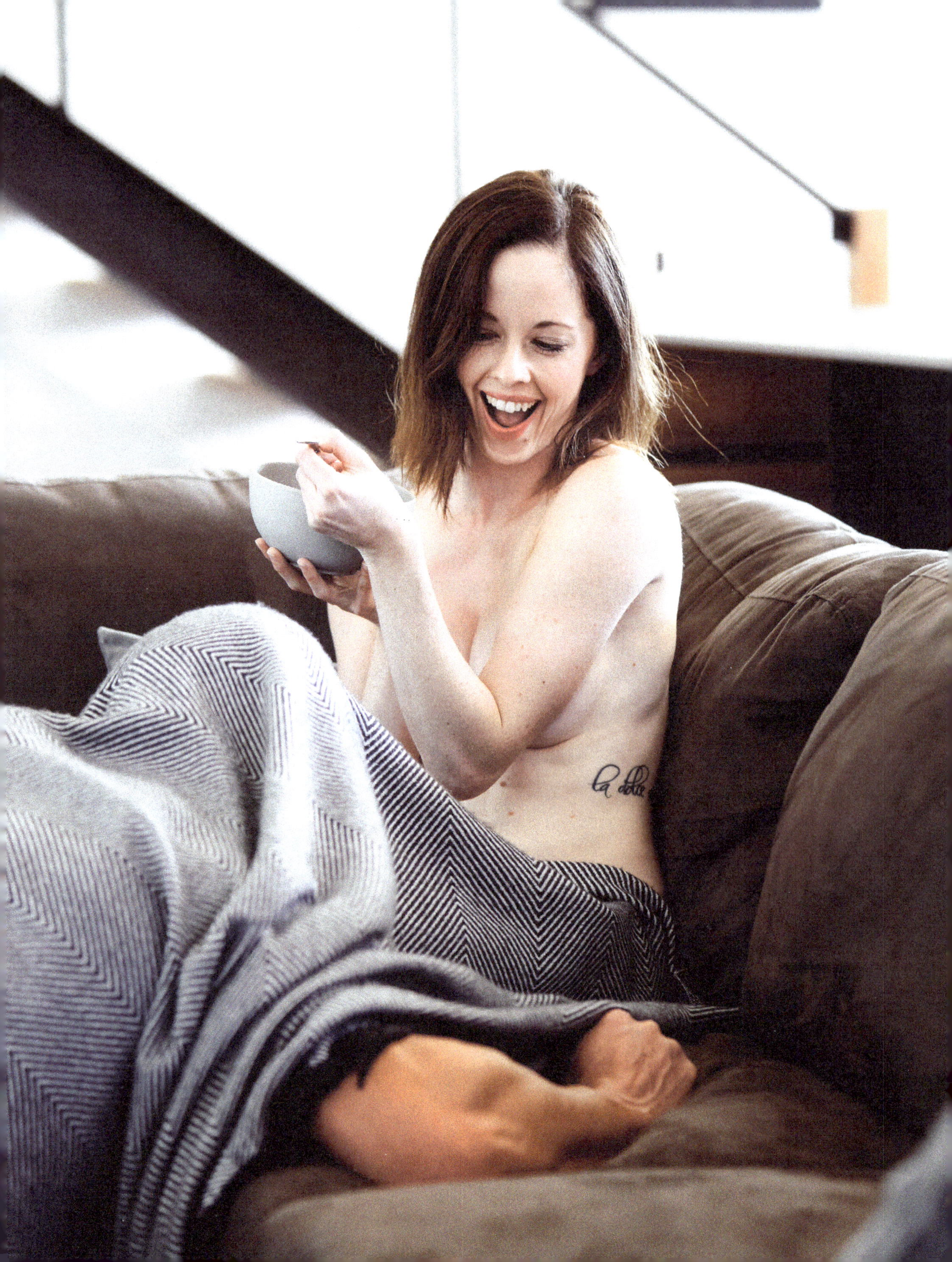

WILD OATS
TOASTED MUESLI

MAKES 8 CUPS

¼ cup rice bran oil
¼ cup honey
¼ cup fresh orange juice
1 tsp vanilla bean extract
4 cups rolled oats
1 cup almonds, crushed
1 cup hazelnuts, crushed
1 cup pepitas
1 cup coconut flakes

Vanilla yoghurt, milk, fresh or grilled seasonal fruit, ground cinnamon and honey, to serve

Full of energy to fuel a morning of adventurous fun. Stored correctly in a cool and dry place the muesli will last for at least 3 months.

1. Preheat oven to 180C. Line 2 oven trays with baking paper.

2. Place a small saucepan over medium heat. Add oil, honey, orange juice and vanilla, and stir until warmed through and honey has melted.

3. Add oats, nuts and pepitas to orange juice mixture and stir to combine. Spread mixture onto prepared oven trays and bake for 20 minutes, stirring halfway through, or until golden brown.

4. Transfer muesli mixture to a large bowl and stir through coconut. Set aside to cool completely, then transfer to an airtight container.

5. Serve muesli with vanilla yoghurt, milk, fresh or grilled seasonal fruit, and top with a dusting of cinnamon and honey, if desired.

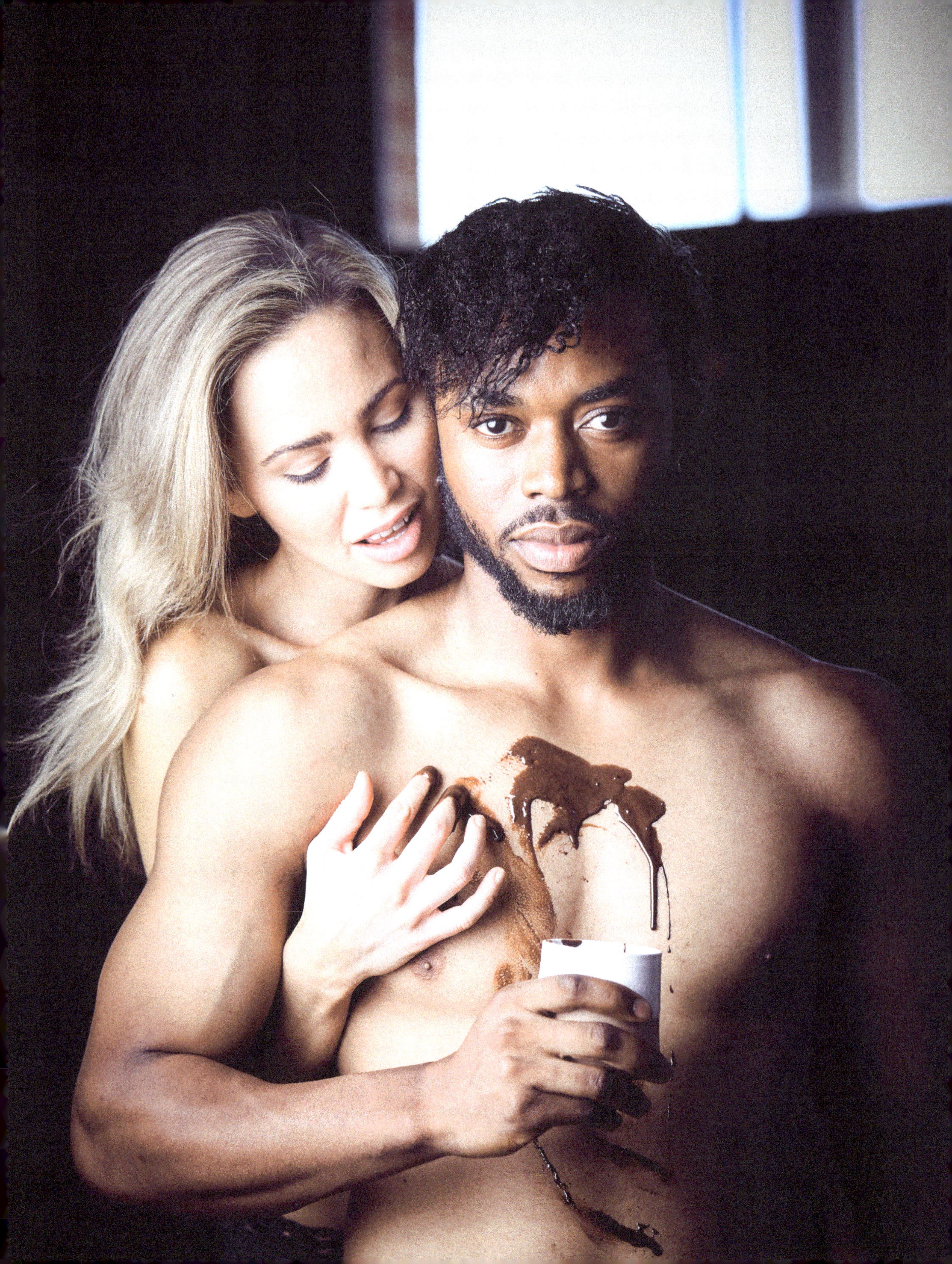

HOT CHOCOLATE

PEANUT BUTTER HOT CHOCOLATE

Salty, sweet and nutty – get cosy and enjoy this soul-warming hot chocolate. Equally as delicious using cow's milk, if you prefer.

SERVES 2

200ml coconut milk
100g dark chocolate (50-70% cocoa solids), chopped
2 tbs smooth peanut butter
1 tbs choc-hazelnut spread

SALTED PEANUT CHOCOLATE

60g dark chocolate (50-70% cocoa solids), chopped
¼ cup roasted, salted peanuts

1. To make salted peanut chocolate, place chocolate in a microwave-safe bowl and heat for 50 seconds. Remove from microwave and stir until all pieces of chocolate have melted. Add peanuts and stir to combine. (You could also stir in some sultanas for a fruit-and-nut combo). Transfer peanut mixture to a small airtight container and place in fridge for 20 minutes or until set. Once set, store at room temperature until ready to serve.

2. To make hot chocolate, place coconut milk in a small saucepan over low heat and bring to a gentle simmer. Add chocolate, peanut butter and choc-hazelnut spread, and stir until combined and chocolate has melted. Pour into glasses and serve with salted peanut chocolate on the side.

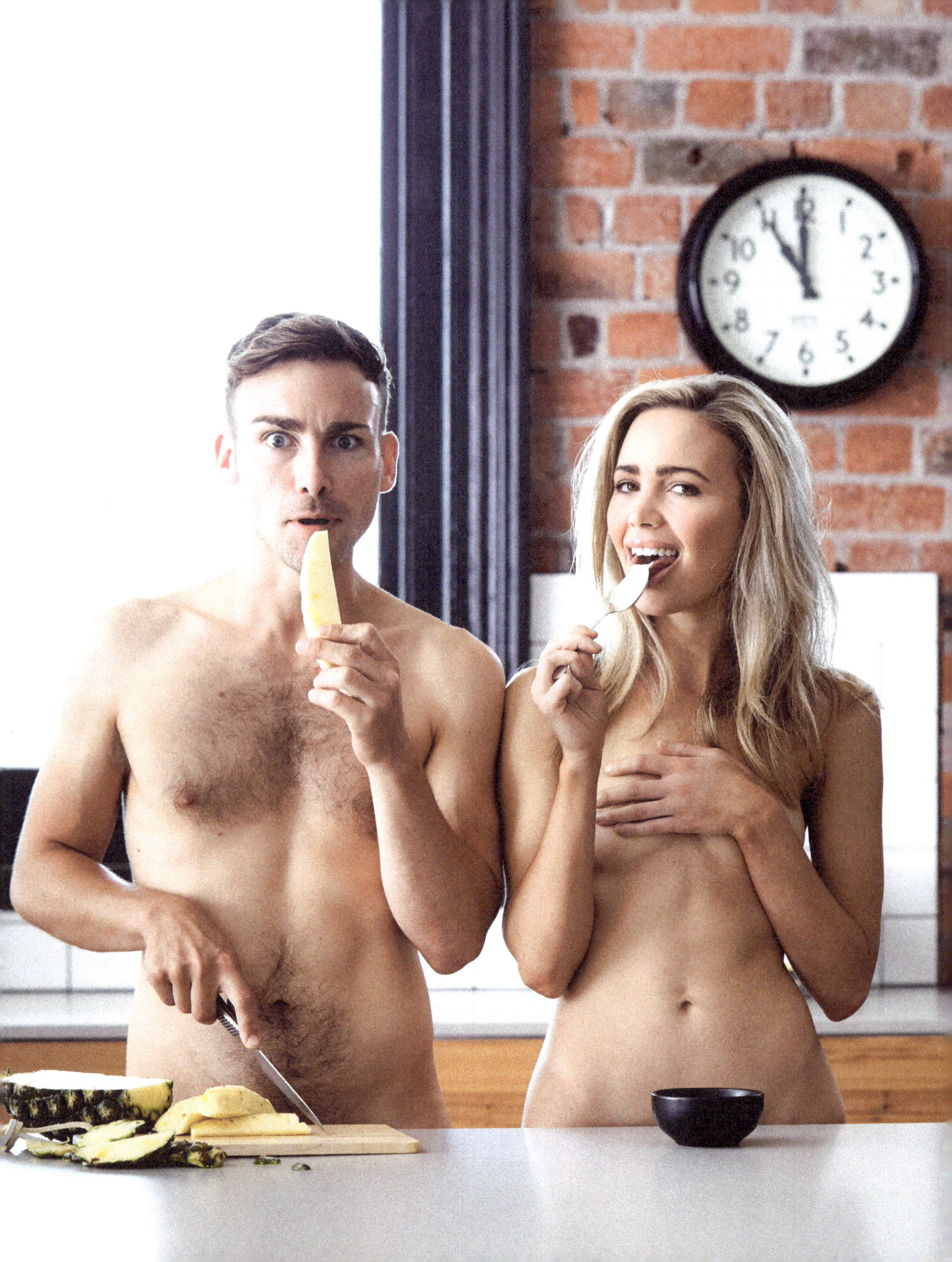

JIZZ IMPROVER
GRILLED PINEAPPLE SALAD

A healthy summer breakfast that's great for improving the flavour within your relationship. Some grilled stone fruits will work just as good with this recipe.

SERVES 3-4

1 cup coconut yoghurt

1 tsp vanilla bean paste

½ pineapple, peeled, cored, cut into long chunks

½ cup toasted coconut flakes

½ cup crushed macadamias

1 lime, zested, juiced

Honey and baby mint leaves, to serve

1. In a small bowl, combine yoghurt and vanilla and set aside in the fridge.

2. Heat a griddle pan over medium-high heat. Add pineapple and grill for 2 minutes each side or until caramelised. Set aside.

3. Smear some yoghurt onto a plate, then layer with pineapple, coconut flakes, macadamias and lime zest and juice. Drizzle with honey and top with mint leaves, to serve.

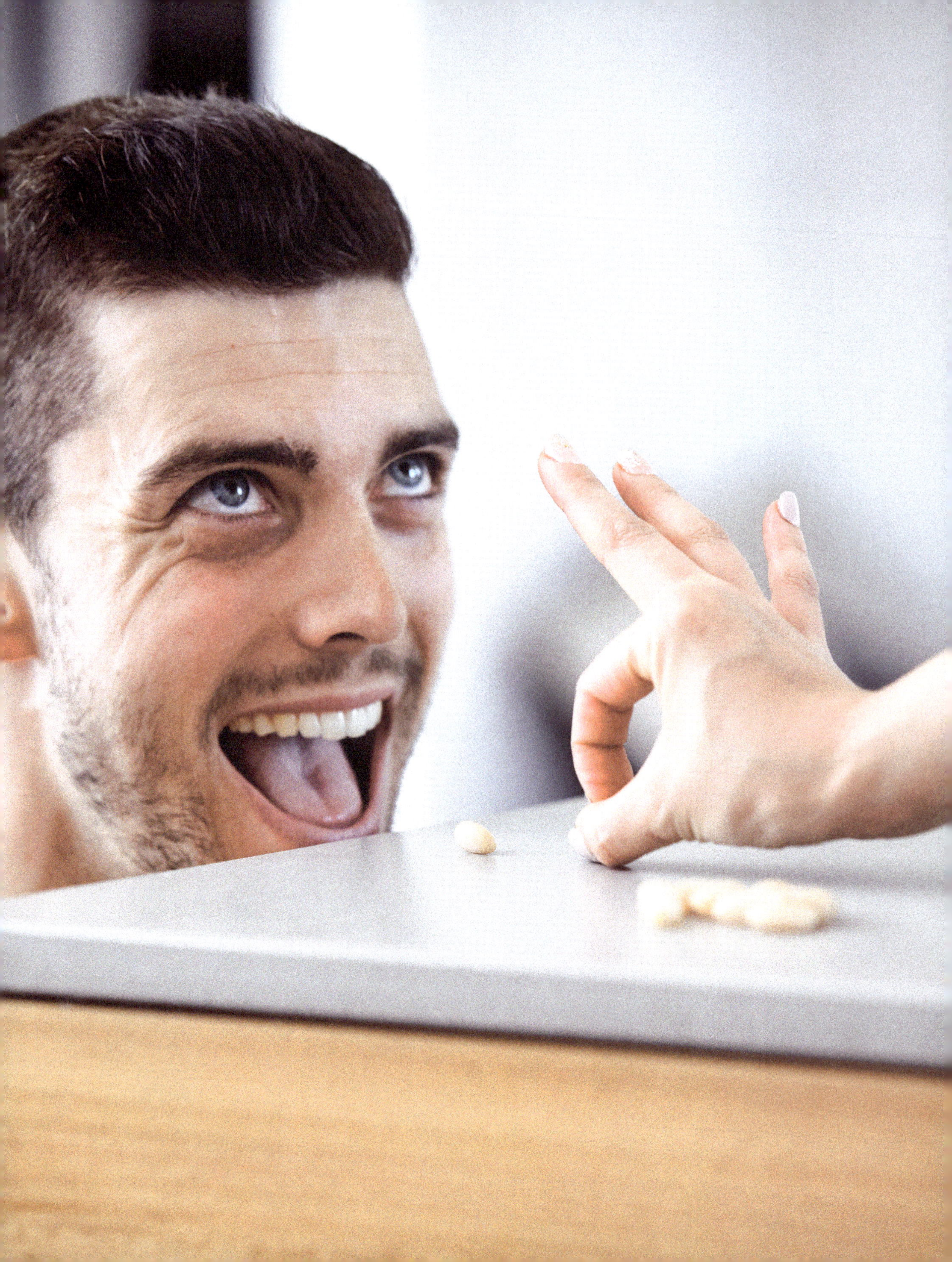

FLICKING THE BEAN

BAKED BEAN JAFFLES

MAKES 4 JAFFLES

Olive oil, to rub
8 slices thick-cut white or wholemeal bread
1 cup grated mozzarella
1 cup grated cheddar cheese
Fresh thyme leaves, to serve

HOMEMADE BAKED BEANS

1 tbs olive oil
4 rashers streaky bacon, trimmed, chopped
1 red onion, halved, sliced
1 carrot, finely chopped
1 garlic clove, finely chopped
1 long red chilli, chopped (seeds removed, if desired)
400g can cannellini beans (juice reserved)
2 thyme sprigs, leaves picked
1 tsp sweet paprika
1 tsp smoked paprika
1 cup tomato passata
1 tbs Worcestershire sauce
1 tsp brown sugar

No need for a knife and fork, just use you hands and enjoy. Try adding fresh baby spinach or rocket to your jaffle for a more wholesome alternative.

1. To make baked beans, preheat oven to 180C. Heat oil in a large high-sided pan over medium-high heat. Add bacon and cook for 2 minutes or until lightly browned. Add onion and carrot and cook for a further 3 minutes or until softened, then add garlic and continue to cook for 2 minutes or until garlic starts to brown slightly.

2. Add chilli, beans with reserved juice, thyme, sweet and smoked paprika along with a generous pinch of salt and pepper. Cook for 2 minutes, then add passata, Worcestershire sauce and sugar. Bring to a simmer, then remove from heat and transfer to a small baking dish. Bake in oven for 15 minutes or until sauce thickens and starts to caramelise slightly. Remove and set aside for 10 minutes, to cool.

3. Rub a little olive oil on one side of each bread slice. On a clean work surface, place bread slices oil-side down and place a generous spoonful of baked beans onto half the bread slices. Sprinkle with mozzarella and cheddar cheeses. Top with remaining slices of bread, oil-side up. Working in batches, grill sandwiches in the jaffle iron until bread is golden brown.

4. Set aside to cool for a few minutes. Sprinkle with thyme leaves, to serve.

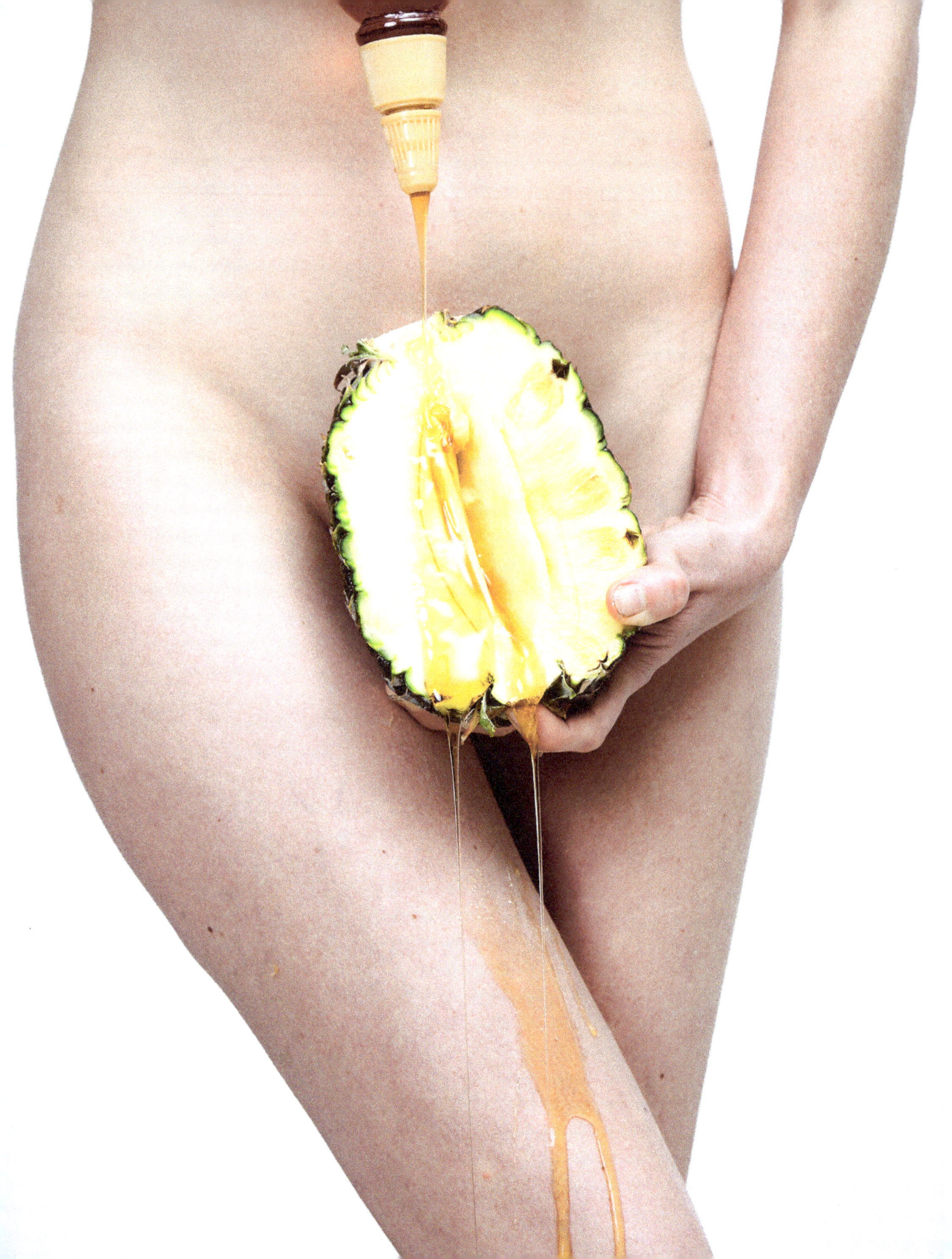

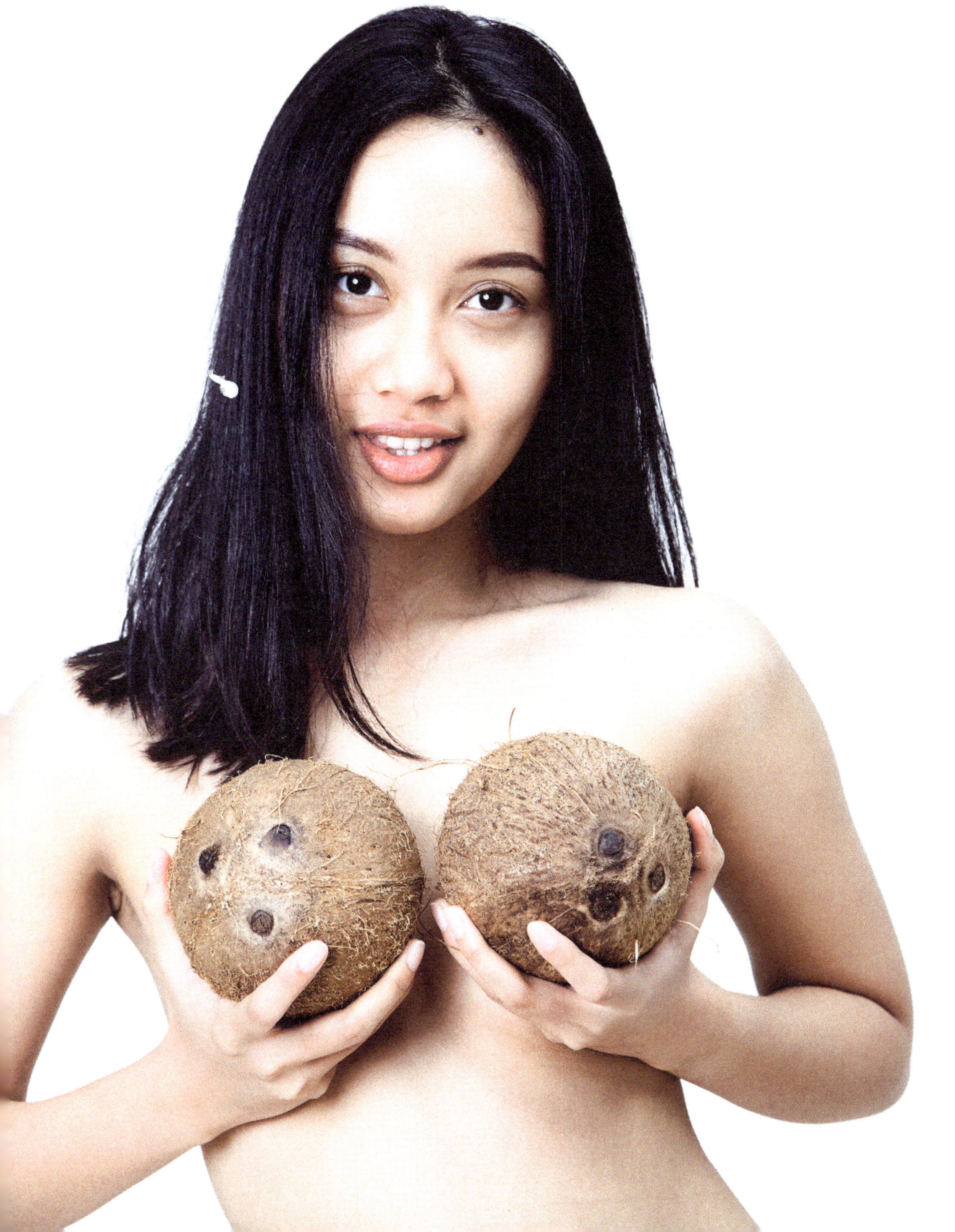

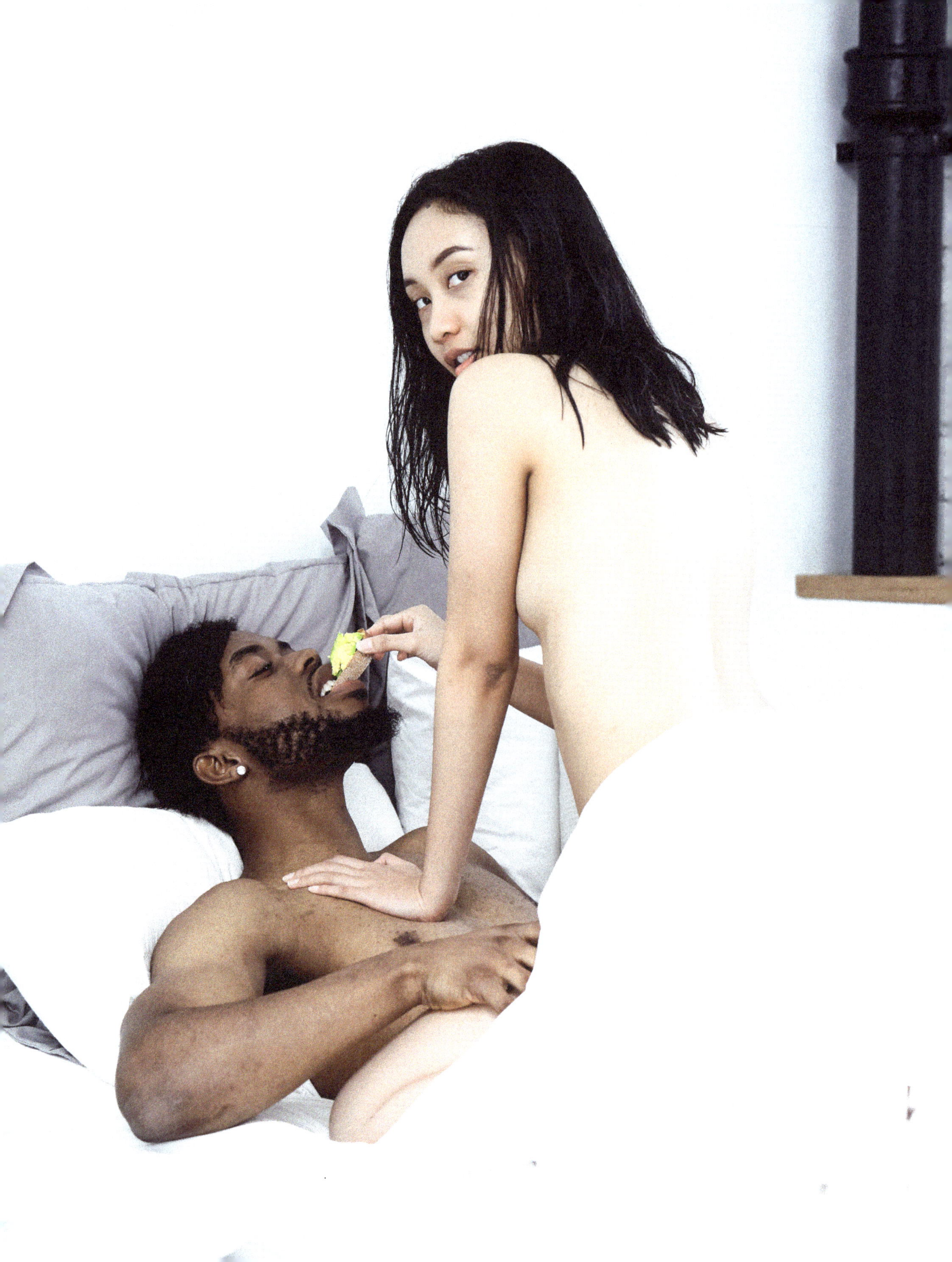

MORNING GLORY

GUACAMOLE TOAST WITH CHORIZO CRUMB

SERVES 3-4

1 ripe avocado, halved, stone removed, peeled
½ jalapeño, finely chopped
1 spring onion, thinly sliced
Handful fresh coriander, chopped
2 tsp olive oil
2 free-range eggs
2 thick slices sourdough, toasted
Fetta, crumbled, to serve

CHORIZO CRUMB

100g hot chorizo
¼ cup pepitas, toasted
1 tsp smoked paprika

This feisty breakfast will add a little spice to your morning. Cook the eggs any way you like.

1. To make guacamole, place avocado flesh into a bowl and roughly mash using a fork. Stir in jalapeño, spring onion and coriander and set aside.

2. To make chorizo crumb, tear and chop chorizo into small chunks. Heat a pan over medium-high heat. Add chorizo and cook for 1 minute or until lightly browned. Add pepitas and cook for a further 2 minutes. Add paprika and stir through for 1 minute or until combined. Remove from heat and set aside.

3. Meanwhile, heat oil in a pan over medium heat. Break eggs into pan and cook for 3-4 minutes, or until cooked to your liking.

4. To serve, top each toast with guacamole, chorizo crumb, fetta and a fried egg.

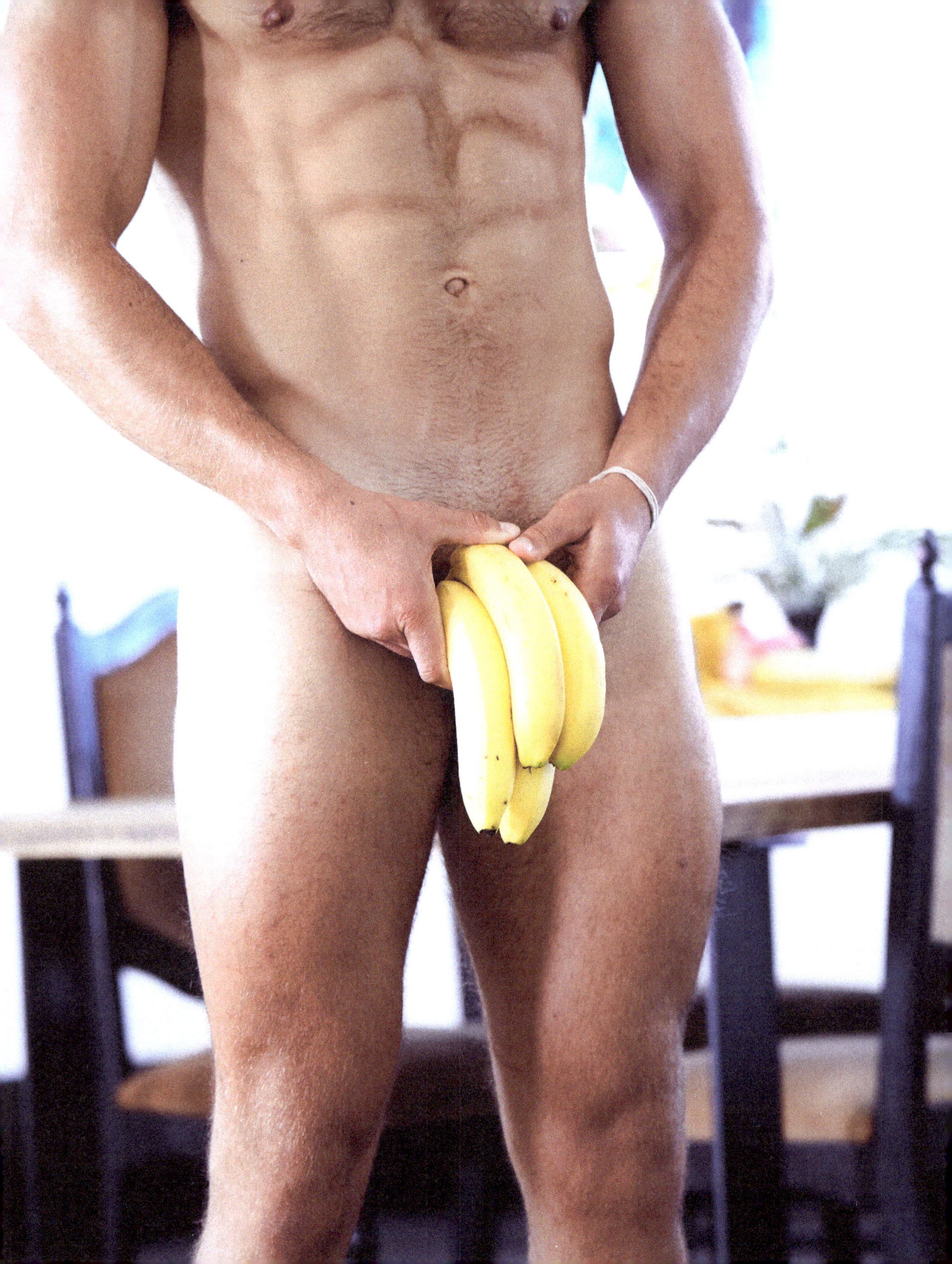

BIG BANANA
BANANA PIKELETS

So plump and delicious you'll want to swallow these bad boys whole. Just as good served with any seasonal fruit you desire.

SERVES 3-4

1 overripe banana
¾ cup milk
1 free-range egg
1 cup self-raising flour
1 ½ tbs caster sugar
Olive oil, to cook
2 bananas, sliced
½ cup crushed roasted hazelnuts
Honey and ground cinnamon, to serve

VANILLA YOGHURT
1 cup Greek yoghurt
1 tbs honey
1 tsp vanilla bean paste to serve

1. To make vanilla yoghurt, combine yoghurt, honey and vanilla in a small bowl. Set aside in fridge.

2. To make pikelet batter, place overripe banana flesh in a mixing bowl and mash with a fork until smooth. Add milk and egg and whisk until combined, then add flour and sugar, and whisk until smooth.

3. Heat oil in a pan over medium heat. Drop large tablespoonfuls of batter into pan and cook for 1 minute or until bubbles appear on the surface. Turn over and cook other side for 1 minute or until golden.

4. To serve, stack pikelets on a plate and top with vanilla yoghurt, sliced banana, hazelnuts, a drizzle of honey and a light dusting of cinnamon.

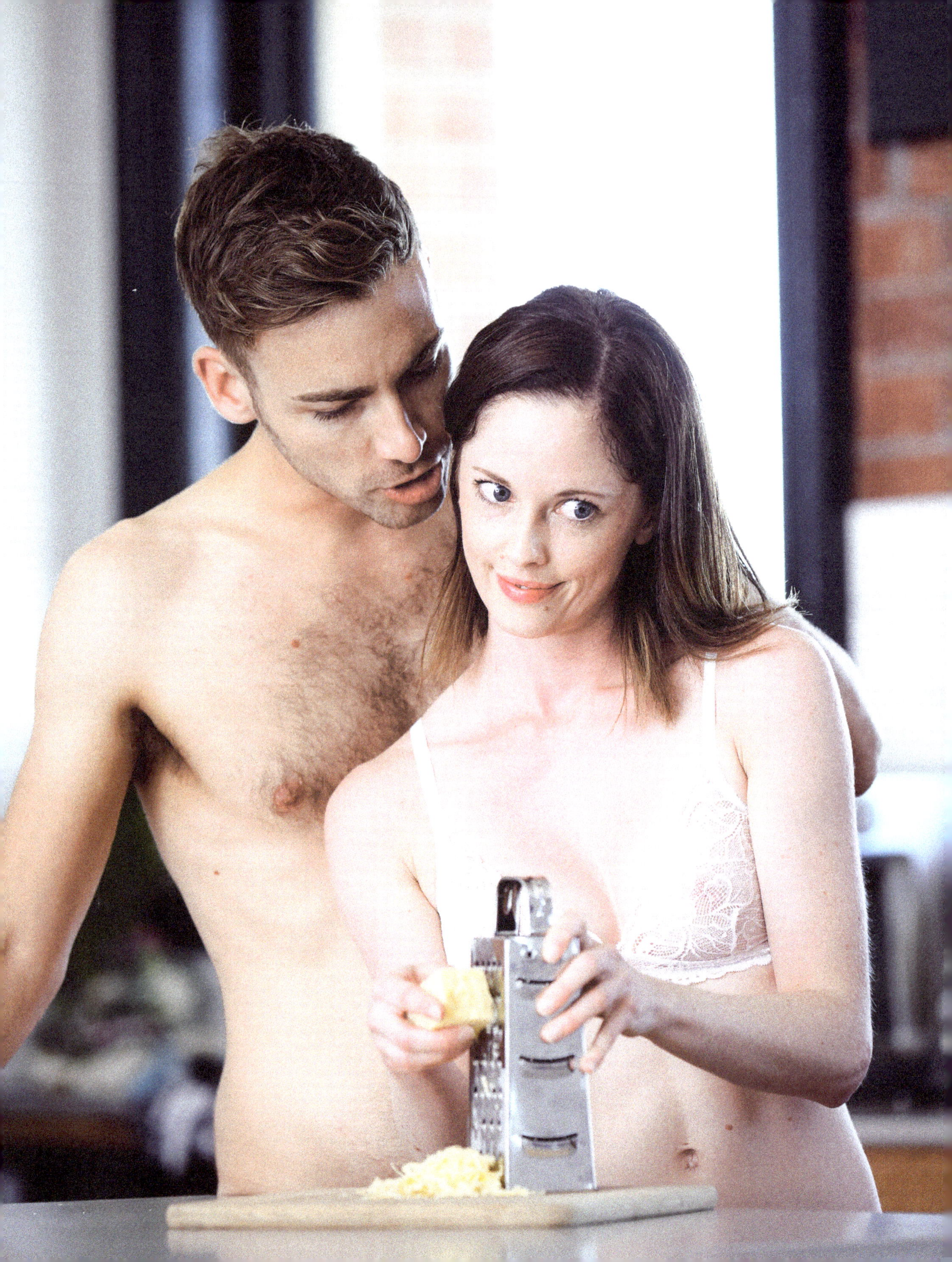

CHEESEY PICK UP
CHEESY TOAST WITH MUSHROOMS

What's your best pick up line? Make this for a loved one and they will crumble like fetta.

SERVES 2

½ cup grated mozzarella
½ cup grated cheddar cheese
2 thyme sprigs, leaves picked
2 handfuls watercress
½ lemon, juiced
⅓ cup olive oil
300g Swiss brown mushrooms, roughly chopped
1 knob butter
1 garlic clove, finely chopped
2 thick slices rye or wholemeal bread
2 cubes goat's fetta, crumbled

1. Combine mozzarella, cheddar and thyme in a small bowl and set aside.

2. Place watercress in a bowl, toss with lemon juice and set aside.

3. Heat oil in a pan over medium-high heat, add mushrooms and cook for 6 minutes or until caramelised. Add butter and garlic, season with a pinch of salt, and cook for a further minute or until garlic is golden brown. Set aside.

4. Toast bread and top with cheese mix and crumbled fetta. Place under grill and cook until cheese is golden and oozy.

5. Season cheesy toast with pepper and serve with mushrooms and watercress.

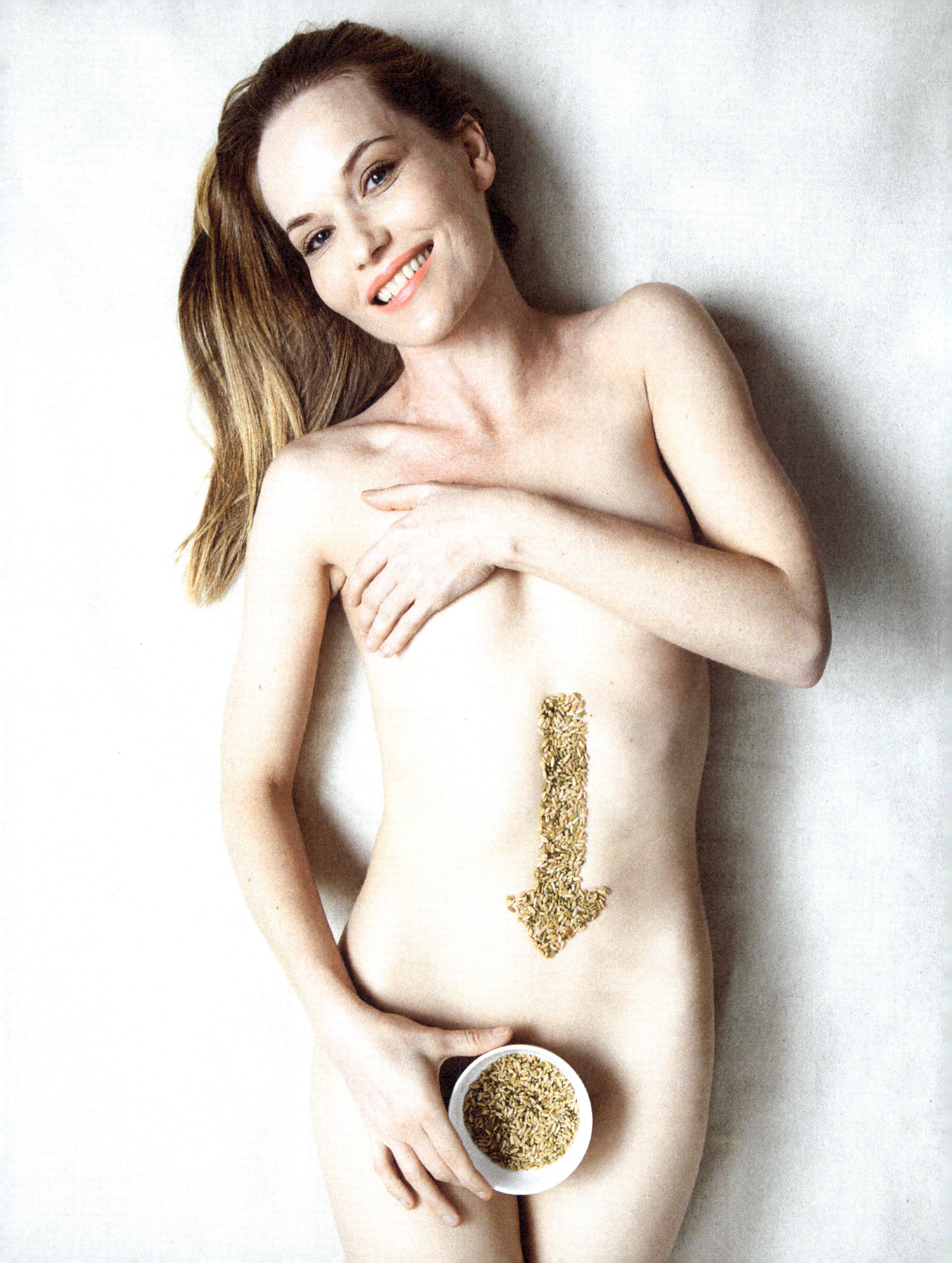

GET YOUR FREEK ON

POACHED EGGS WITH FREEKEH, GREENS AND DUKKAH

SERVES 3-4

½ cup freekeh (roasted green wheat grains)

2 cups chicken or vegetable stock

2 tbs olive oil, plus extra, to brush

½ red onion, finely chopped

2 garlic cloves, finely chopped

1 lemon wedge, juiced

4 broccolini stems

4 asparagus spears

2 free-range eggs

2 tsp white vinegar

DUKKAH

½ cup roasted hazelnuts

½ cup roasted almonds

½ cup sesame seeds, toasted

½ cup coriander seeds

1 tbs. black pepper

1 tbs cumin seeds

1 tsp sea salt

½ tsp chilli flakes

Perfect breakfast or brunch for the health nymphos out there. This recipe makes extra dukkah – store in an airtight container in the cupboard for up to 2 months.

1. To make dukkah, place all ingredients into a food processor and process to a fine crumb. Set aside.

2. Place freekeh in a small pot with stock over medium heat. Bring to a simmer, then reduce heat to low, cover and cook for 40 minutes or until al dente. Drain and set aside.

3. Heat oil in a pan over medium heat. Add onion and garlic and cook for 3-4 minutes or until golden. Add cooked freekeh and toss until heated through. Remove from heat and squeeze over lemon juice. Season to taste with a pinch of salt and pepper.

4. Lightly brush broccolini and asparagus with extra oil, and grill on a griddle pan over high heat for 2 minutes each side or until lightly charred. Roughly chop greens, then toss them through the freekeh mix.

5. Meanwhile, bring a small pot of water with vinegar to the boil. Reduce heat to low so water is still simmering gently. Using a wooden spoon, stir water to create a whirlpool. Crack each egg into the centre of the pot. Cook for 2-3 minutes for a soft yolk, or 3-4 minutes for a firmer yolk. Using a slotted spoon, remove egg from water and set aside. Repeat with remaining egg.

6. Serve poached eggs on top of freekeh salad and sprinkle over a generous amount of dukkah.

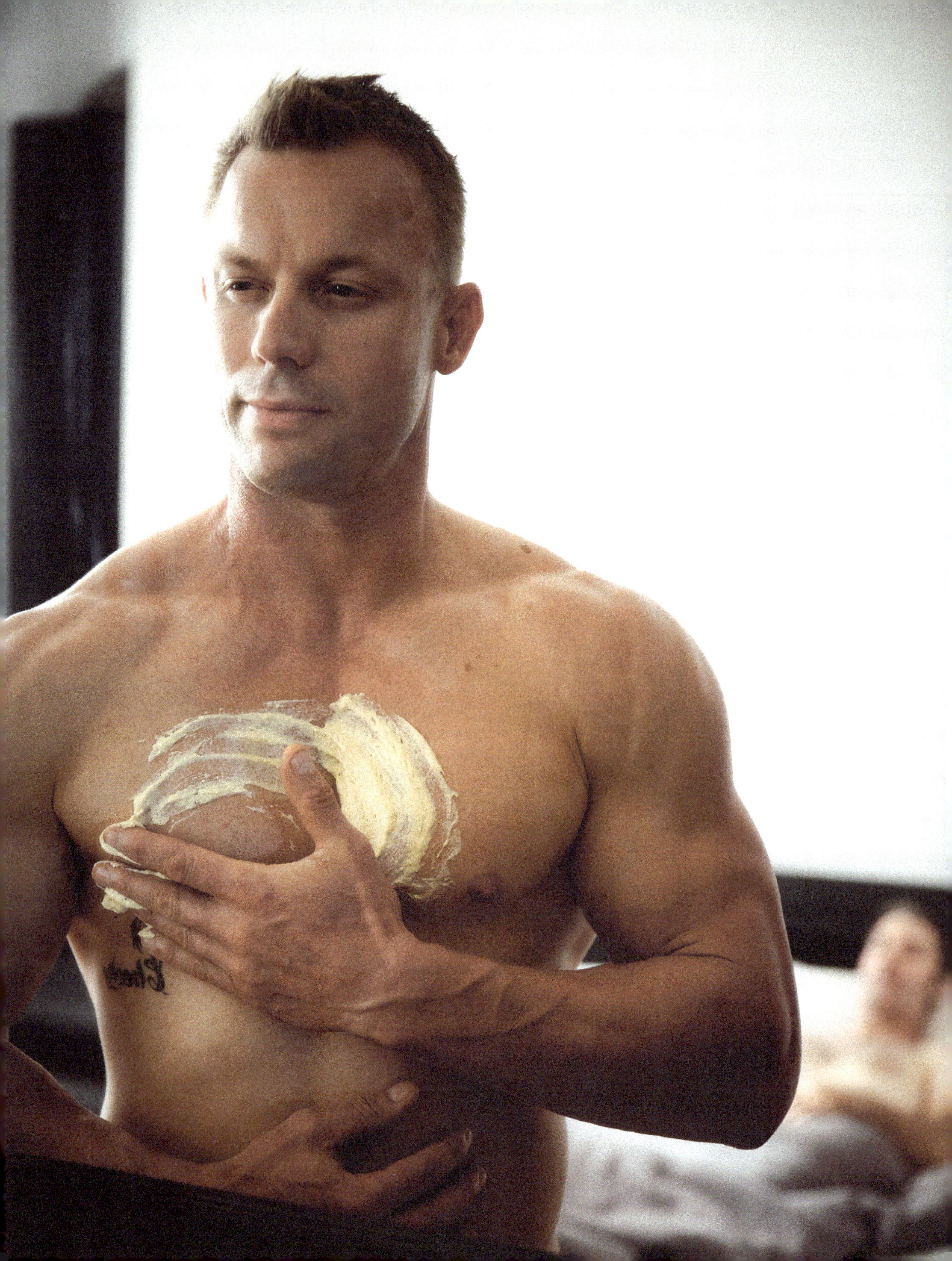

HUMMUSEXUAL

HUMMUS WITH SMOKY HARISSA

If you're going to rub this recipe all over your body, just beware of the chilli around sensitive areas. Start this recipe a day ahead. The hummus and harissa are best left to develop flavours overnight.

MAKES 2 CUPS HUMMUS AND 1/2 CUP HARISSA

Turkish bread

Olive oil and chopped flat-leaf parsley, to serve

HUMMUS

1 garlic clove, unpeeled

⅓ cup light olive oil, plus extra, to drizzle

400g can chickpeas, drained, rinsed

1 tbs tahini

½ lemon, juiced

HARISSA

3 garlic cloves, unpeeled

1 red capsicum

3 dried long red chillies (for a milder result, use less chillies)

½ tsp cumin seeds

½ tsp coriander seeds

1 tsp smoked paprika

1 tsp sweet paprika

1 tsp salt

½ tsp cracked black pepper

1 tbs olive oil, plus extra to coat

1. Preheat oven to 200C. Place unpeeled garlic for hummus and harissa on a baking tray, drizzle with a little olive oil and roast for 10-15 minutes or until golden brown. Remove from oven, peel and set aside.

2. To make hummus, place 1 roasted garlic clove in a food processor with remaining ingredients and season with a good pinch of salt. Process until smooth then season to taste if required (if hummus is too thick, add a little water to thin slightly). Place in an airtight container and set aside in fridge until ready to serve.

3. To make harissa, char capsicum over a gas burner or charcoal grill, turning, until blackened all over. Transfer to a bowl covered with plastic wrap and set aside until cool enough to touch. Remove and discard burnt skin, stem and seeds, then roughly chop capsicum flesh.

4. Meanwhile, soak chillies in a bowl of hot water for 15 minutes. Remove and discard stalks, and roughly chop chillies.

5. Toast cumin and coriander in a hot dry pan for 2 minutes or until fragrant (be careful not to burn them). Using a mortar and pestle, grind cumin, coriander, paprika, salt and pepper to a rough powder.

6. Place all harissa ingredients, including 3 remaining roasted garlic cloves, into a small food processor or blender and process to a coarse paste. Place in an airtight container, smooth surface and top with a thin layer of oil. Set aside in fridge until ready to serve.

7. Toast or grill Turkish bread and cut into lengths to use as dippers. To serve, top hummus with harissa, drizzle with oil and garnish with parsley. Serve with Turkish bread dippers. Alternatively, you could chop up some fresh crunchy vegetables.

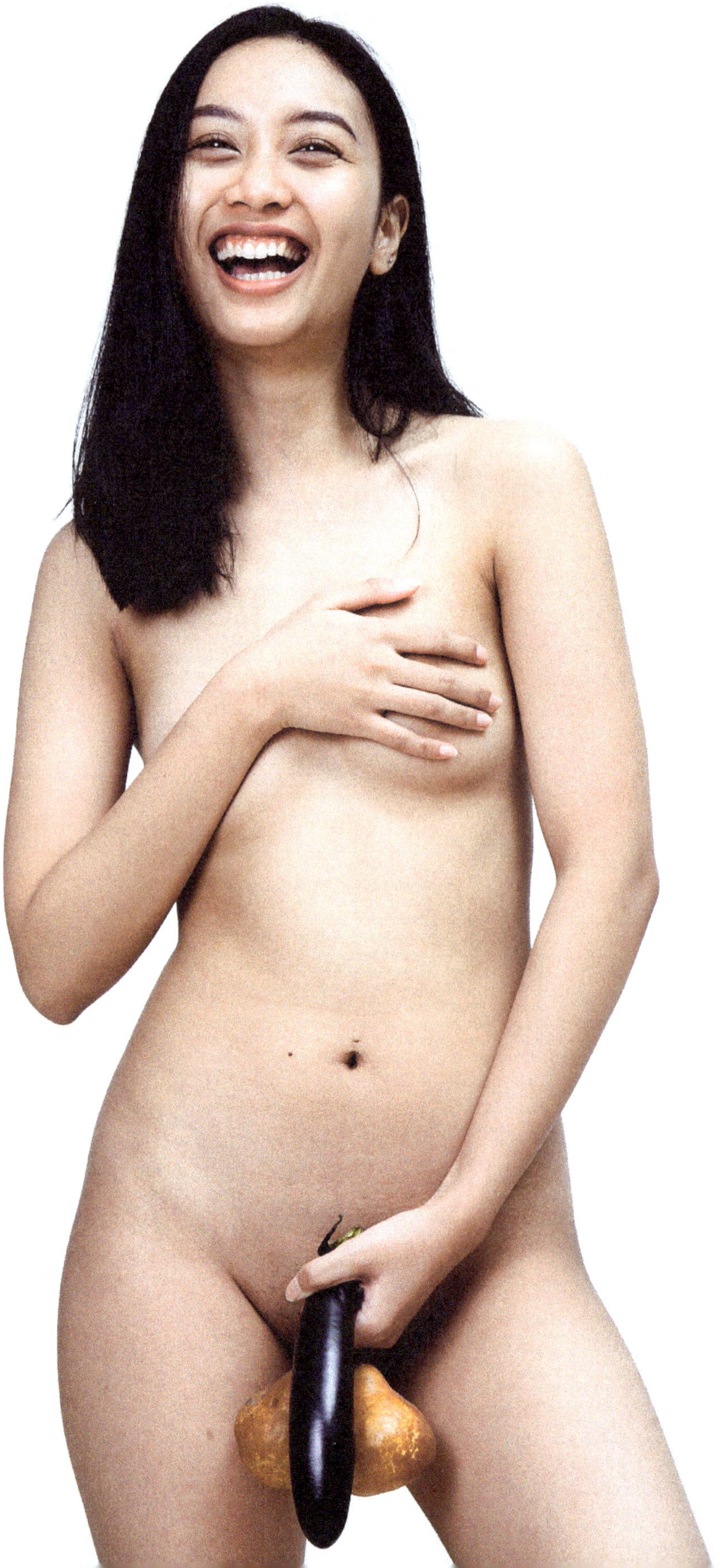

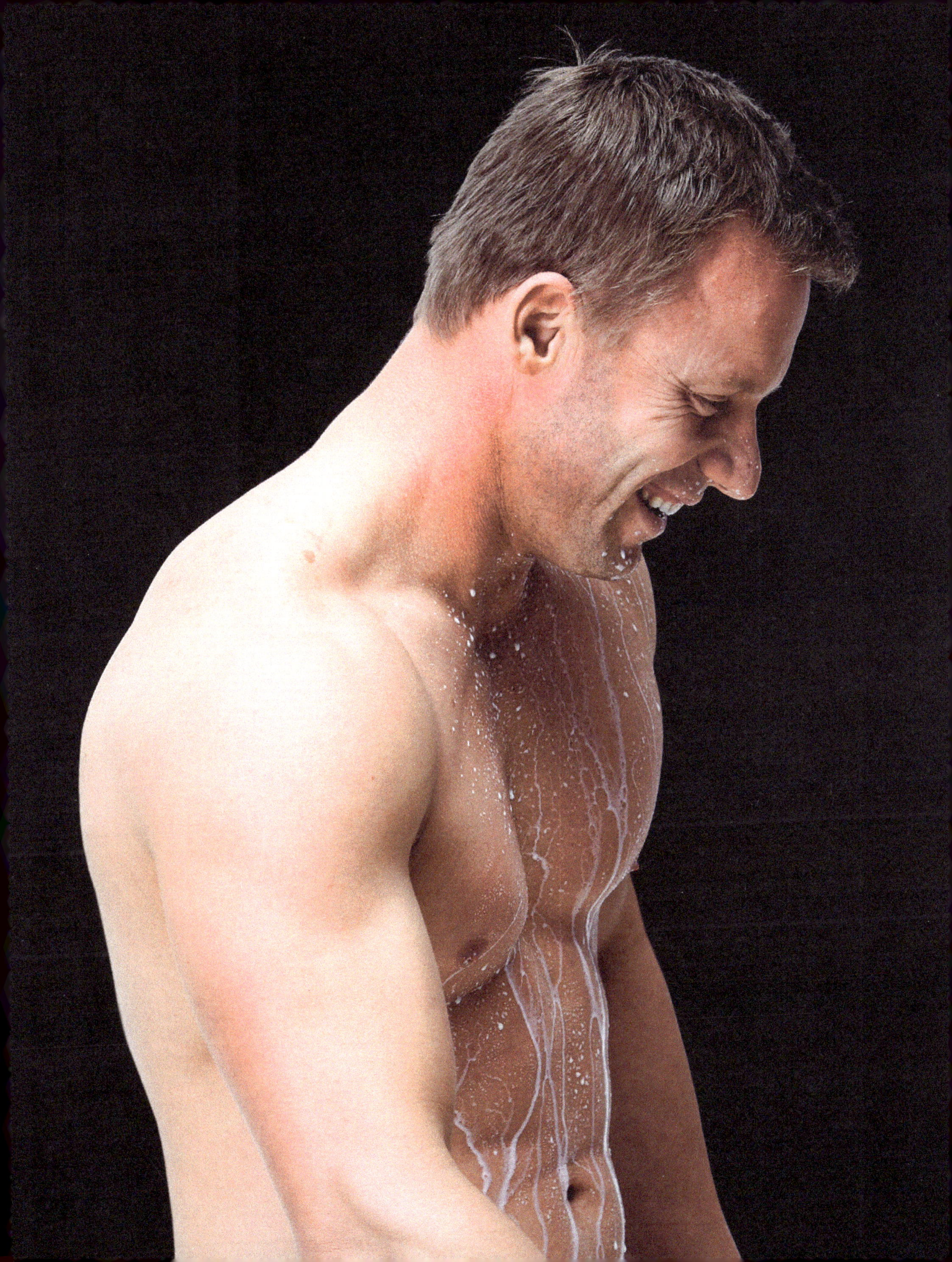

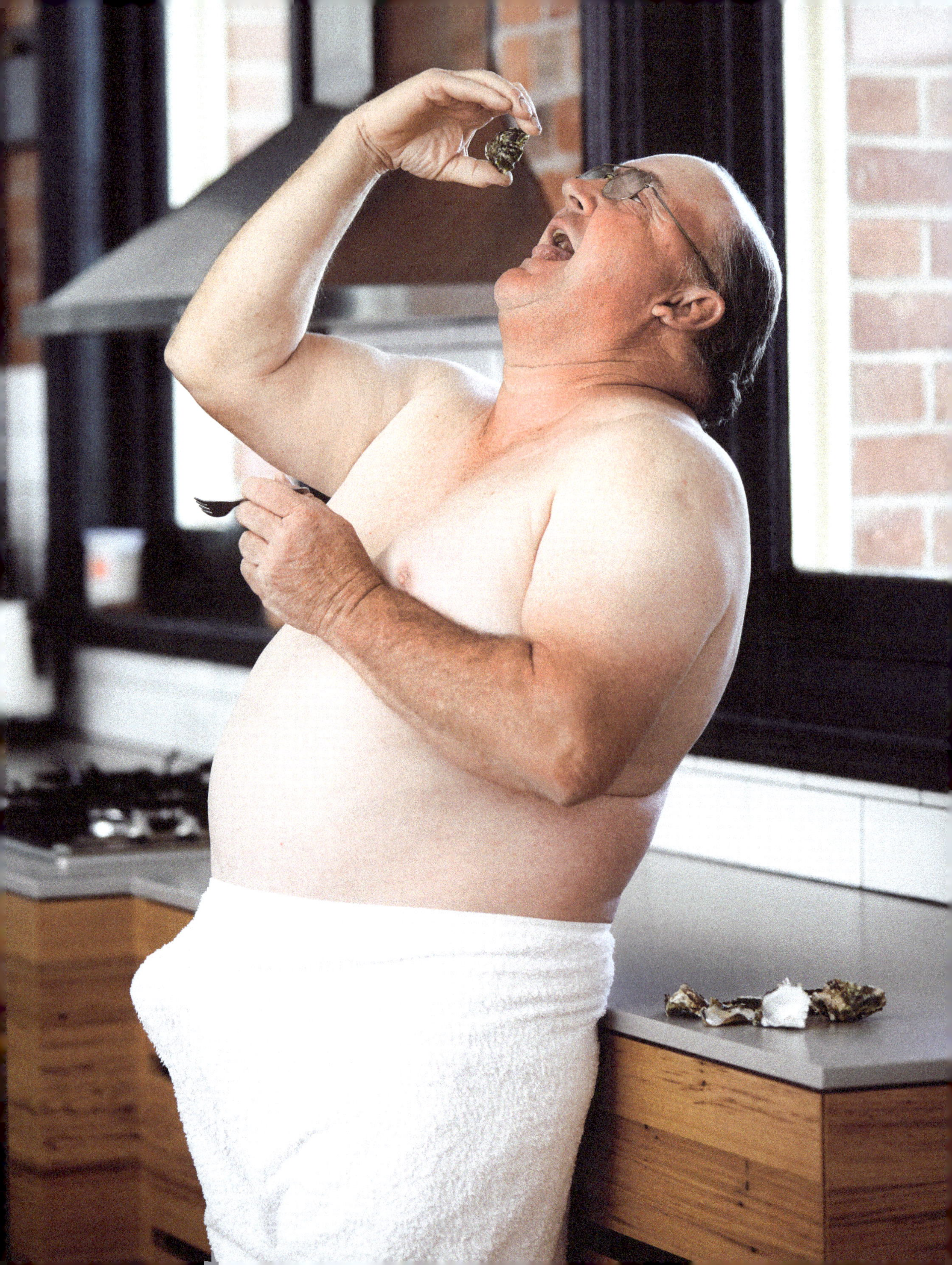

APHRODISIAC

NATURAL OYSTERS WITH SHALLOT DRESSING

SERVES 4 AS A STARTER

24 freshly shucked natural oysters
2 tsp palm sugar, finely grated
5 tbs red wine vinegar
2 tbs finely chopped shallots
Tabasco sauce and mixed micro herbs, to serve

This dish will rise to any occasion. If you can't track down the micro herbs, just use a little chopped dill or chervil.

1. To make shallot dressing, place sugar and vinegar in a small bowl and stir until sugar dissolves. Stir in shallots and season with salt. Set aside for 15 minutes for flavours to develop.

2. To serve, spoon a little shallot dressing over each oyster, top with a dash of Tabasco sauce and garnish with micro herbs.

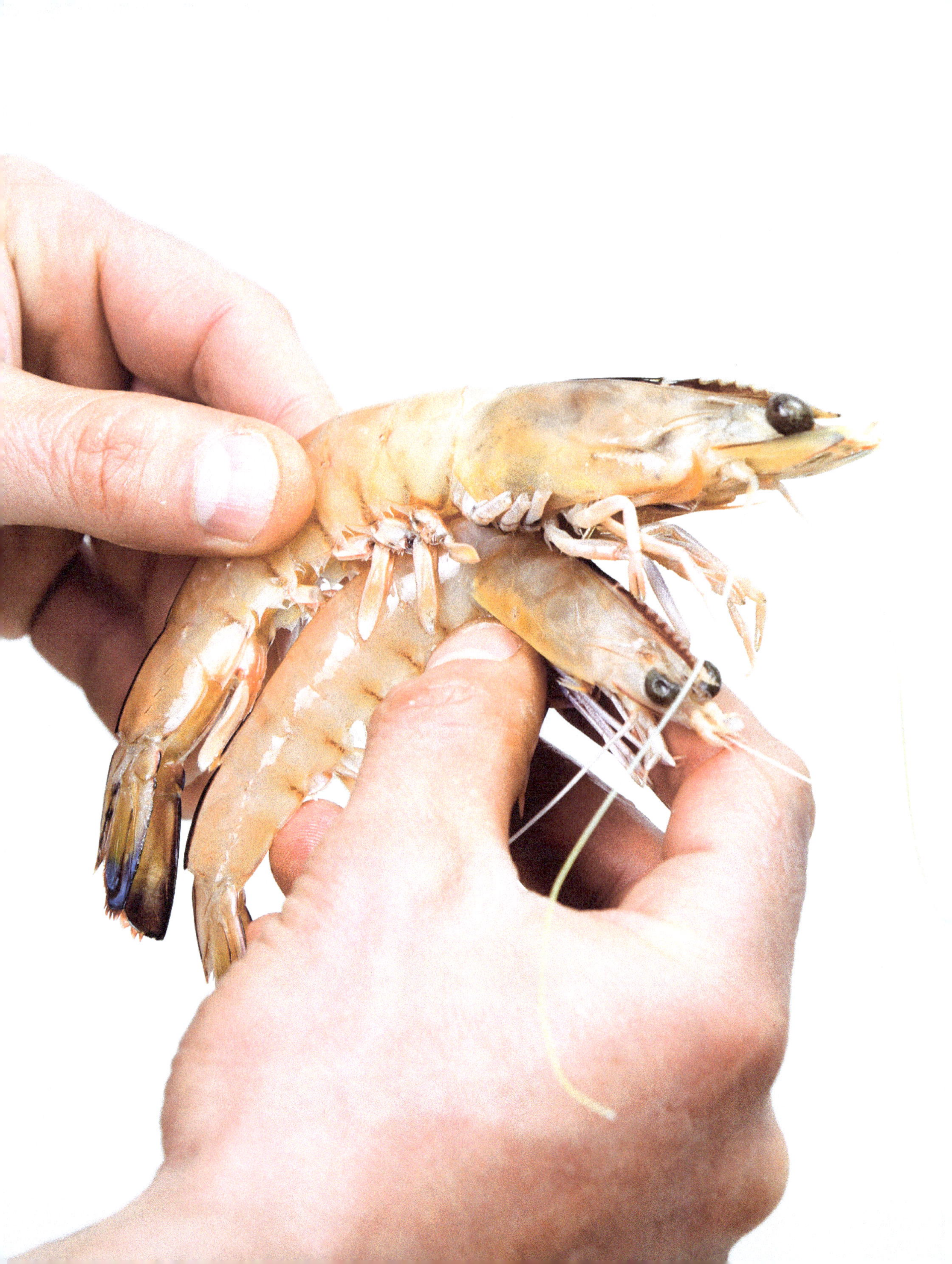

PRAWN STARS

CHILLI AND GARLIC PRAWNS

Throw on some Barry White and embrace your inner porn star while preparing these tasty morsels. Serve as a side dish or throw them on top of a steak for your ultimate surf 'n' turf.

SERVES 5 AS A SIDE

2 tbs olive oil
20 large raw king prawns, peeled (tails intact), deveined
5 garlic cloves, finely chopped
1 tbs sambal oelek
1 tbs butter
Handful parsley, chopped
Lemon wedges, to serve

1. Heat oil in a wok over high heat. Add prawns and stir-fry for 1-2 minutes or until half cooked. Add garlic, sambal oelek and butter. Stir-fry for a further minute or until garlic is golden and prawns are just cooked through.

2. Remove from heat and toss through parsley. Serve with lemon wedges.

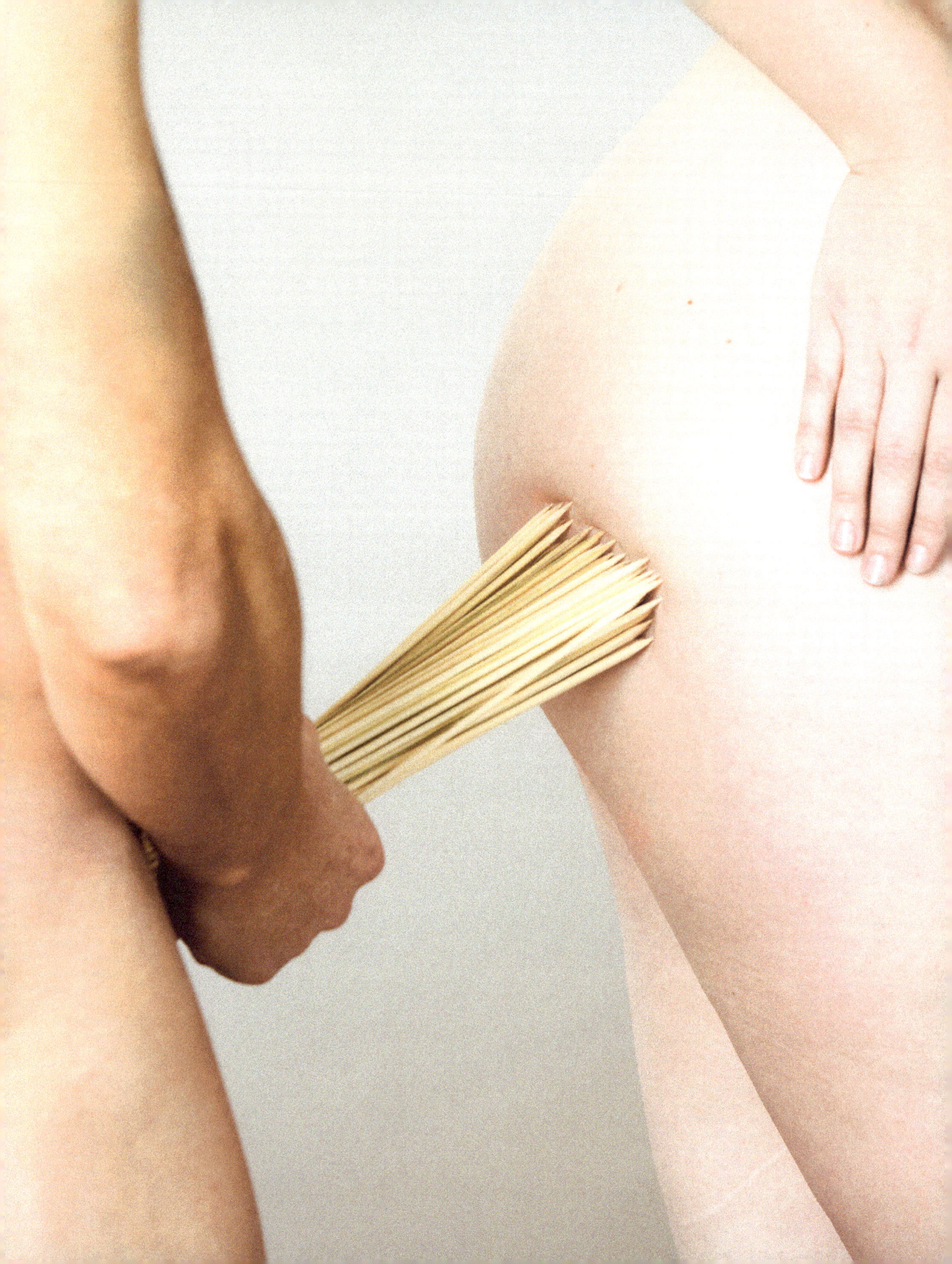

STICK IT TO ME

CHICKEN SATAY SKEWERS WITH CUCUMBER SALAD

SERVES 4

12 small wooden skewers
6 free-range chicken thigh fillets, cut into bite-size chunks
1 tsp ground turmeric
2 tbs peanut oil
1 cup roasted, unsalted peanuts
1 cup coconut milk
½ lime, juiced
2 tbs soy sauce
1 tbs palm sugar
Fried shallots, to garnish

PASTE

2 long red chillies (use 1 for less heat)
½ red onion, roughly chopped
2cm cube ginger
1cm cube galangal
1cm cube fresh turmeric
2 garlic cloves, roughly chopped
2 coriander roots, roughly chopped
½ lime, zested
4 tbs peanut oil

SALAD

2 small Lebanese cucumbers, roughly chopped
1 carrot, thinly sliced
Handful fresh mint leaves
Handful fresh coriander leaves
1 tbs lime juice
1/2 tbs palm sugar
1 tbs of water
1 tsp sambal oelek

These meat sticks are an oral delight. Serve with steamed rice for a complete meal. Soak skewers overnight to prevent burning.

1. Place chicken into a bowl. Add turmeric, 1 tbl of soy sauce and peanut oil, toss to coat, then cover and place in fridge for at least 30 minutes to marinate, preferably overnight.

2. Place peanuts into a food processor and process to a coarse crumb. Alternatively, crush peanuts in batches using a mortar and pestle. Set aside.

3. To make paste, place all ingredients in a food processor or blender and process to a coarse paste. Use a mortar and pestle, if you prefer. Set aside.

4. To make salad, place cucumber, carrot, mint and coriander in a bowl and toss together. In a small jar place lime juice, palm sugar, water and sambal then seal and shake until sugar has dissolved. Toss salad with dressing just before serving.

5. Heat wok over medium heat, add paste and cook for 3 minutes or until fragrant and lightly caramalised. Add crushed peanuts, coconut milk, lime juice, soy sauce and palm sugar and stir until combined and heated through.

    Add extra soy sauce, palm sugar or lime juice until ideal balance between sweet, sour and salty is achieved. Keep warm on a very low heat until ready to serve.

6. Meanwhile, thread chicken onto skewers (use gloves to avoid turmeric staining hands). Place on a barbecue or griddle pan over high heat and cook for 5 minutes each side or until cooked through. Serve skewers topped with satay sauce and fried shallots, and with salad on the side.

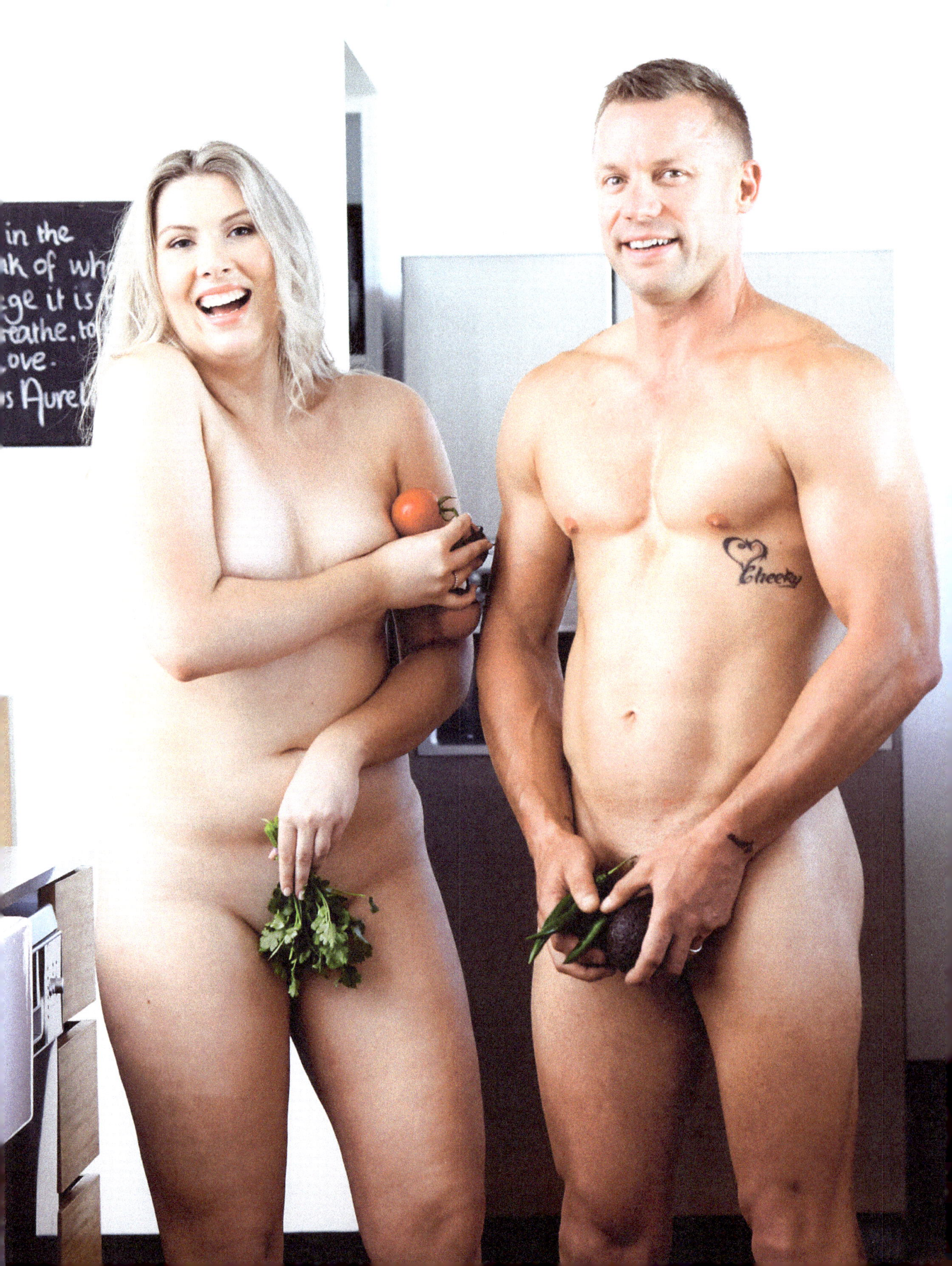
in the
Cheeky

IN THE RAW
CEVICHE

Get naked in the kitchen and embrace the rawness with this deliciously fresh canapé. I used a combination of both Kingfish and Tuna.

SERVES 10 AS A CANAPÉ

500g sashimi-grade tuna or kingfish, thinly sliced
20 round corn chips
1 avocado, halved, stone removed, peeled, diced
1 large ripe tomato, deseeded, diced
1 green chilli, thinly sliced
Coriander leaves, to serve

CURING LIQUID
75ml lemon juice
75ml lime juice
1 tbs palm sugar, finely grated
2 coriander roots, finely chopped
1 tbs finely chopped shallots
1 tsp fresh ginger, cut into julienne
1 tsp fish sauce

1. Combine all curing liquid ingredients in a bowl and stir until sugar has dissolved completely. Gently place fish into liquid, making sure every piece is covered, then set aside for 10 minutes to cure. Drain and serve immediately.

2. To serve, place cured fish on a large platter with corn chips, avocado, tomato, chilli and coriander. Arrange ceviche components on top of corn chips as desired.

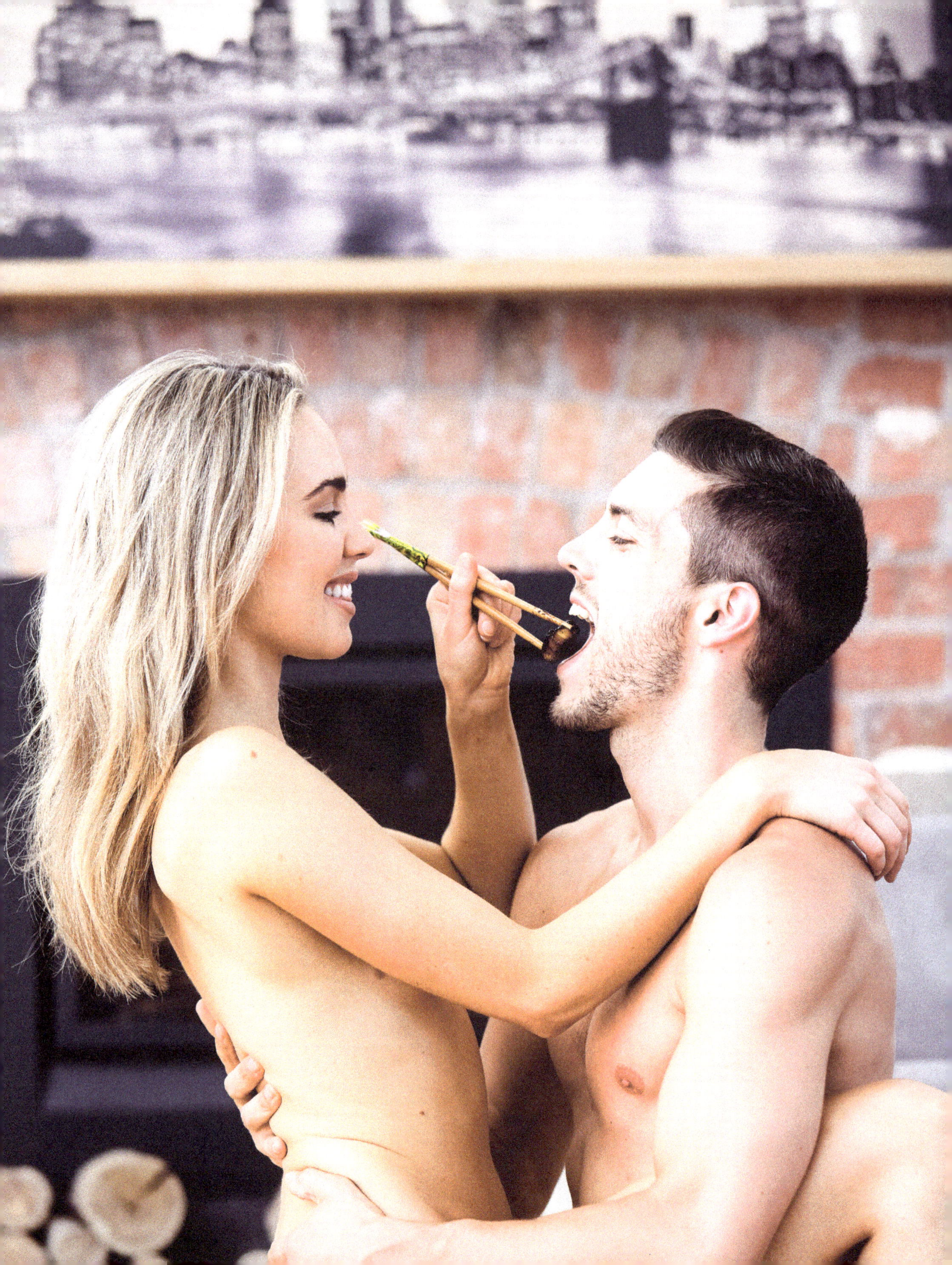

PORK ME

PORK SPARE RIBS WITH APPLE AND FENNEL SLAW

Feed this to your partner for some super soft pork action. Start this recipe a day ahead.

1 star anise
Thumb-size piece ginger
2 garlic cloves
½ red onion, chopped
2 tsp pepper
1 tsp chilli flakes
2 tbs red wine vinegar
2 tbs ketjap manis
1 tbs fish sauce
6 pork spare ribs (approximately 600g), skin-on
1 tbs honey
Ketjap manis and chilli flakes, to serve

PICKLED CHILLIES

100ml white wine vinegar
1 tsp salt
1 tbs caster sugar
2 long red chillies, thinly sliced

APPLE AND FENNEL SLAW

1 green apple, cored, cut into julienne
1 small fennel bulb, thinly sliced
Handful fresh coriander, chopped
½ lime, juiced

1. To make marinade, using a mortar and pestle grind star anise to a powder. Add ginger, garlic and onion and bash to a coarse paste. Add pepper, chilli, vinegar, ketjap manis and fish sauce, and stir until combined.

2. Coat spare ribs with marinade then place in an airtight container and refrigerate overnight. Remove from fridge 30 minutes before cooking.

3. To make pickled chillies, heat vinegar, salt and sugar in a small saucepan and stir until sugar has dissolved. Pour liquid over sliced chillies, seal in an airtight container and set aside in fridge.

4. When ready to cook, preheat oven to 140C. Wrap spare ribs in baking paper, then wrap and seal in foil. Place in a heavy-based roasting pan and bake for 3 hours.

5. Remove baking paper and foil, return ribs to roasting pan and drizzle with honey. Increase oven to 220C and bake for a further 15 minutes or until lightly caramelised and sticky. Remove from heat and set aside to rest for 5 minutes.

6. Meanwhile, to make apple and fennel slaw, place apple, fennel and coriander in a bowl and toss with lime juice.

7. To serve, cut spare ribs into a chunky dice, drizzle with ketjap manis, sprinkle over chilli flakes and serve with pickled chillies and apple and fennel slaw.

* Ketjap Manis is a sweet soy sauce available from most supermarkets.

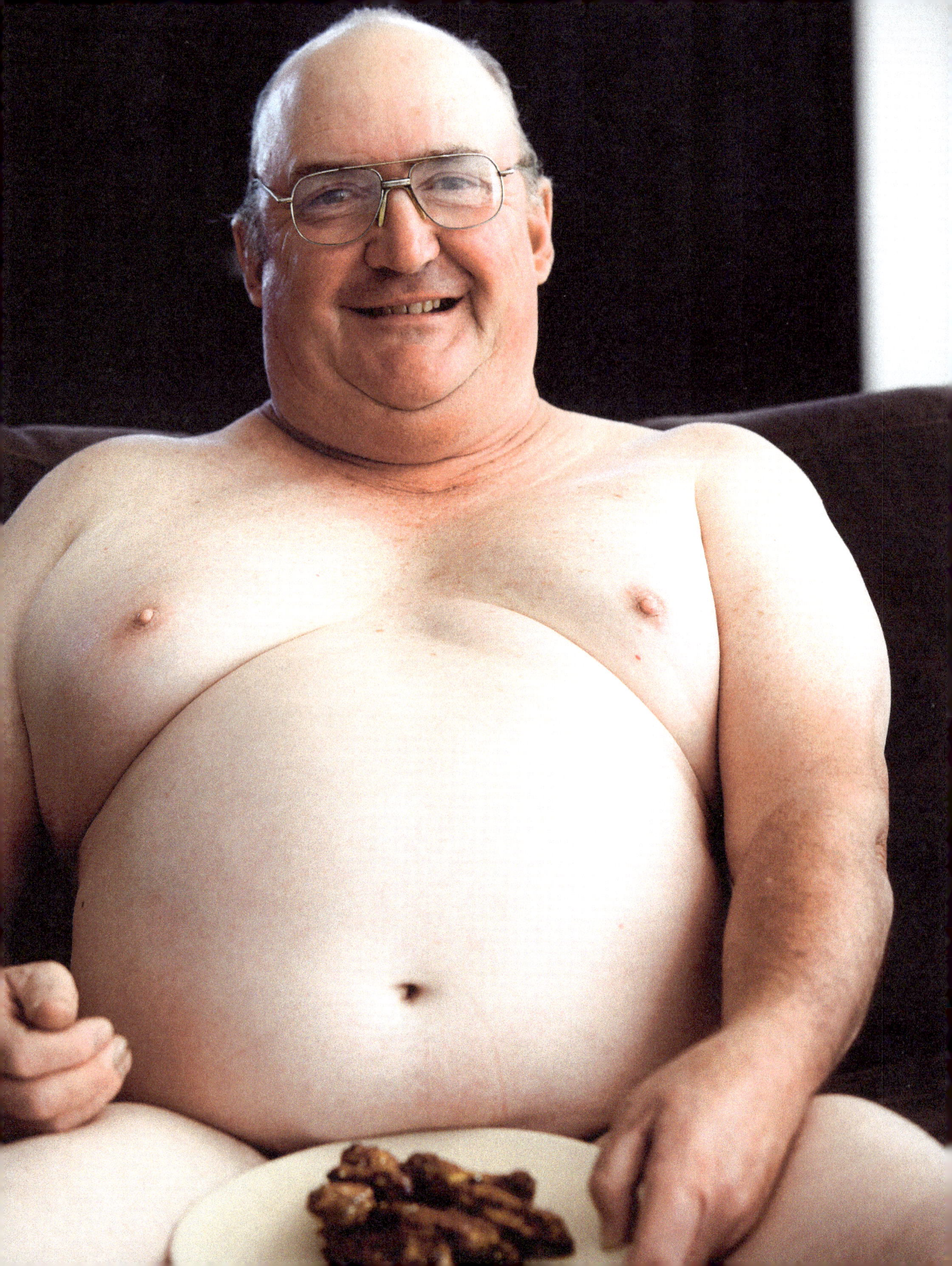

STICKY FINGERS

HONEY CHILLI CHICKEN WINGS

You'll be licking your fingers clean after trying these moreish little treats.

SERVES 10 AS A CANAPÉ

1 tsp fennel seeds
1 tsp coriander seeds
1 tsp black peppercorns
1 tsp smoked paprika
1 tsp salt
2 tbs olive oil
1 tbs balsamic vinegar
20 chicken wings, halved, tips removed
Juice of ½ a lemon
2 tbs honey
1 tbs sesame seeds, toasted
Handful fresh coriander, roughly chopped
2 tsp chilli flakes (optional)

1. Preheat oven to 180C. Using a mortar and pestle, grind fennel, coriander and peppercorns to a coarse powder, then place in a large bowl with paprika, salt, oil, vinegar and chicken wings. Toss to coat.

2. Transfer to a large oven tray lined with baking paper and bake for 45 minutes or until wings are crisp and caramelised.

3. Remove from oven and toss wings in lemon juice, honey, sesame seeds, coriander and chilli flakes. Serve.

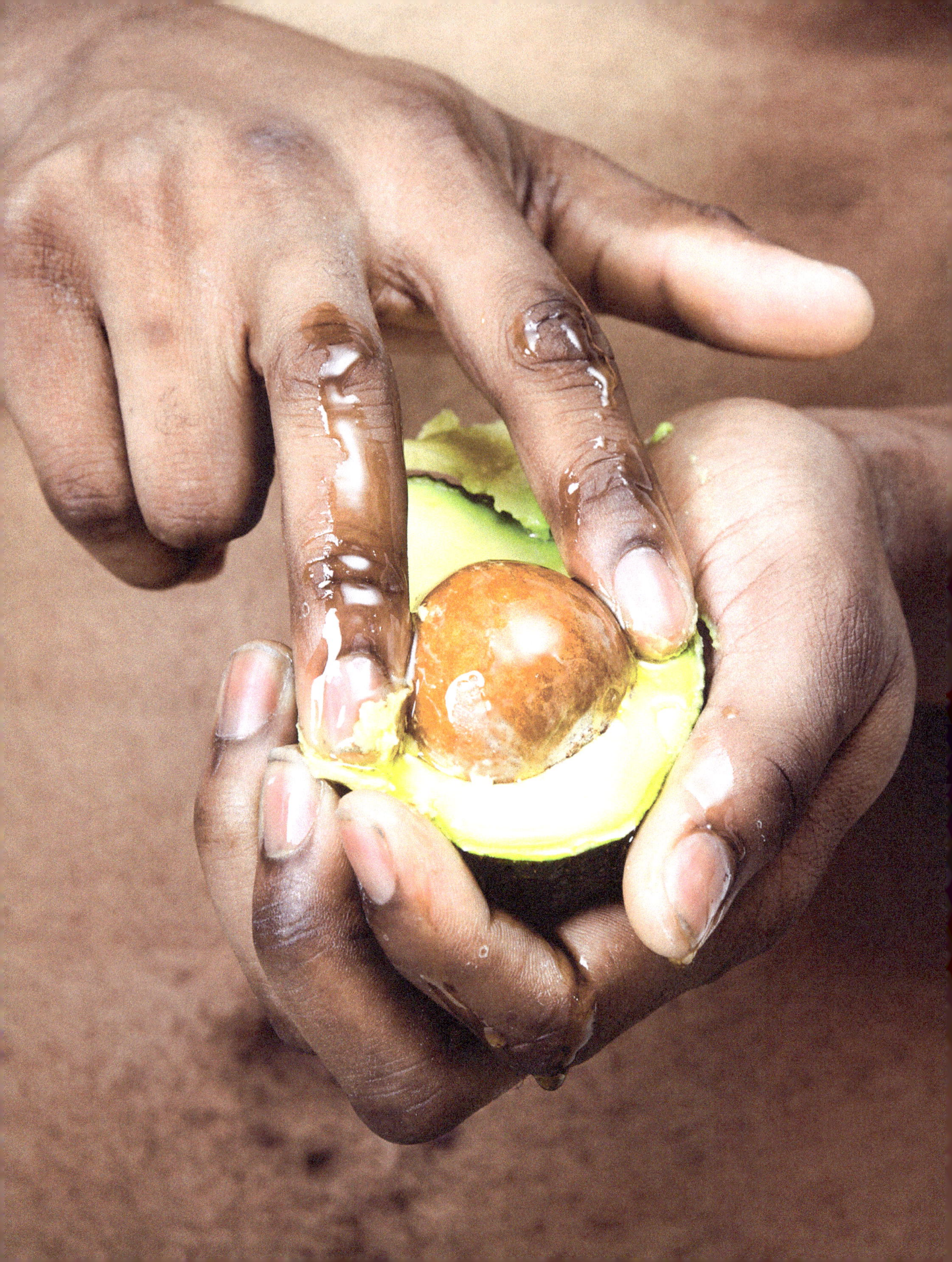

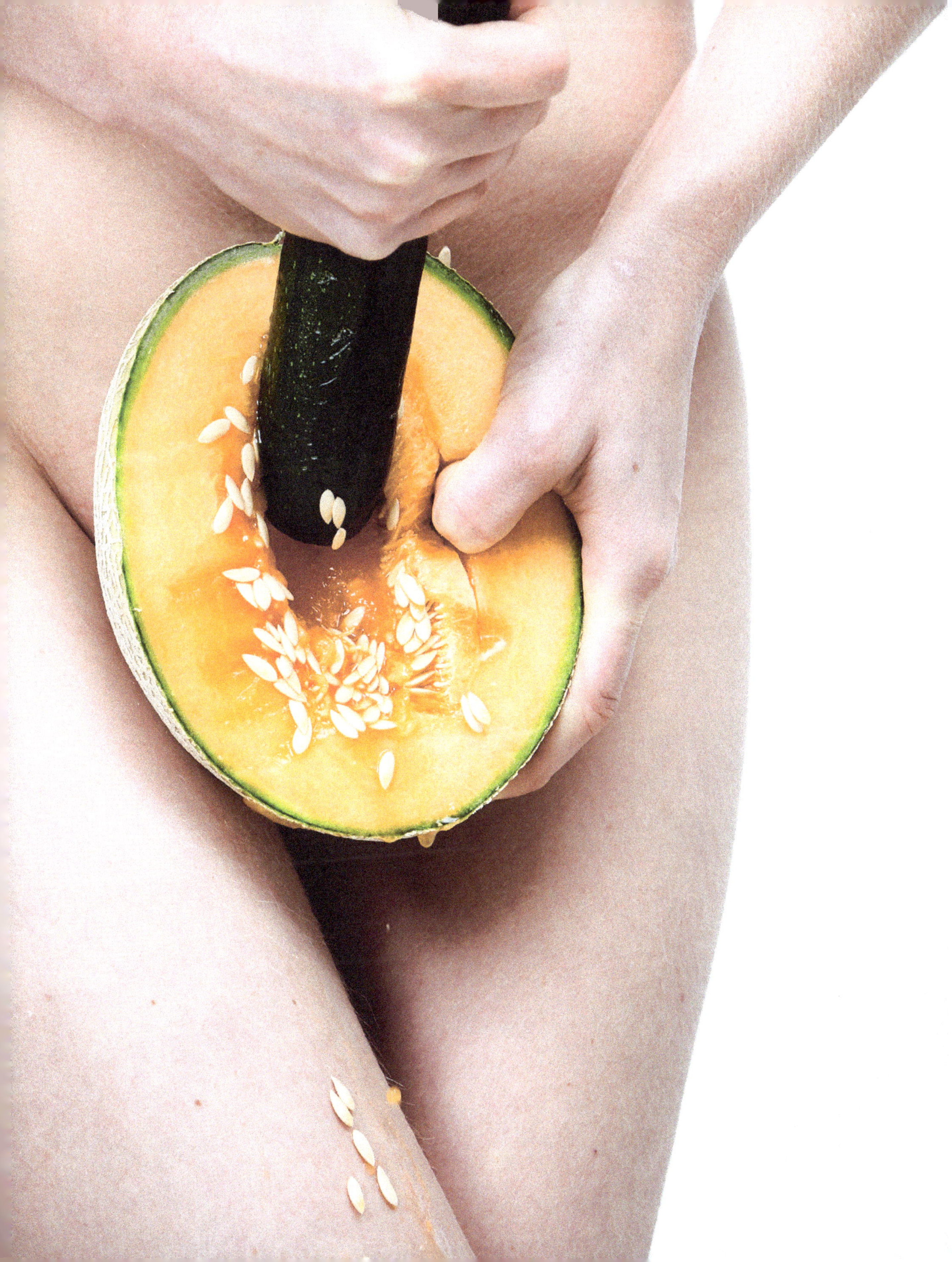

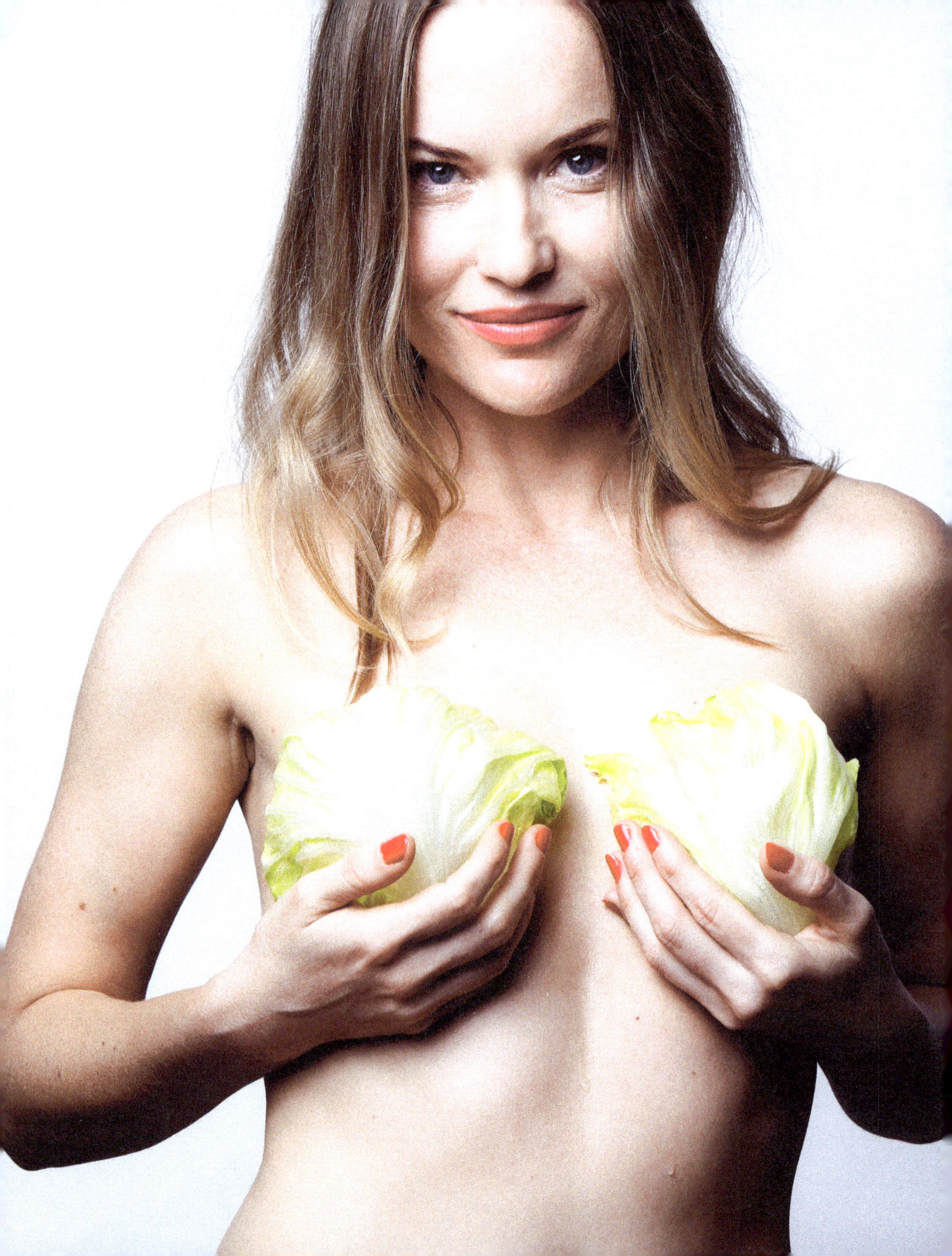

C-CUPS

CHICKEN SAN CHOI BAU

Fresh, tasty handfuls of goodness. Pork mince could also be used, alternatively increase the amount of mushroom for a vegetarian version.

SERVES 4

- *2 tbs olive oil*
- *1 large field mushroom, finely chopped*
- *1 carrot, finely chopped*
- *1 celery stalk, finely chopped*
- *1 red onion, finely chopped*
- *½ thumb-size piece ginger, finely grated*
- *2 garlic cloves, finely chopped*
- *500g chicken mince*
- *1 iceberg lettuce, washed, leaves separated into cup shapes*
- *1 long red chilli, finely chopped*
- *2 handfuls bean sprouts*
- *1 bunch fresh coriander, cut into sprigs*
- *Fried shallots, lime wedges and soy sauce, to serve*

SAN CHOY BAO SAUCE

- *½ lime, juiced, plus extra, to season*
- *1 tbs oyster sauce*
- *1 tbs ketjap manis, plus extra, to season*
- *1 tbs fish sauce*
- *1 tsp sesame oil*

1. To make sauce, combine all ingredients in a small bowl and set aside.

2. Heat oil in a wok over medium-high heat, add mushroom, carrot, celery and onion and stir-fry for 2 minutes, then add ginger and garlic and stir-fry for a further 3 minutes or until garlic is golden. Add chicken and stir-fry until cooked through. Stir through sauce and adjust flavour using extra lime juice or ketjap manis if required. Transfer to a serving bowl.

3. To serve, fill lettuce cups with chicken, and top with chilli, sprouts, coriander and shallots. Squeeze over lime and drizzle with soy sauce, if desired.

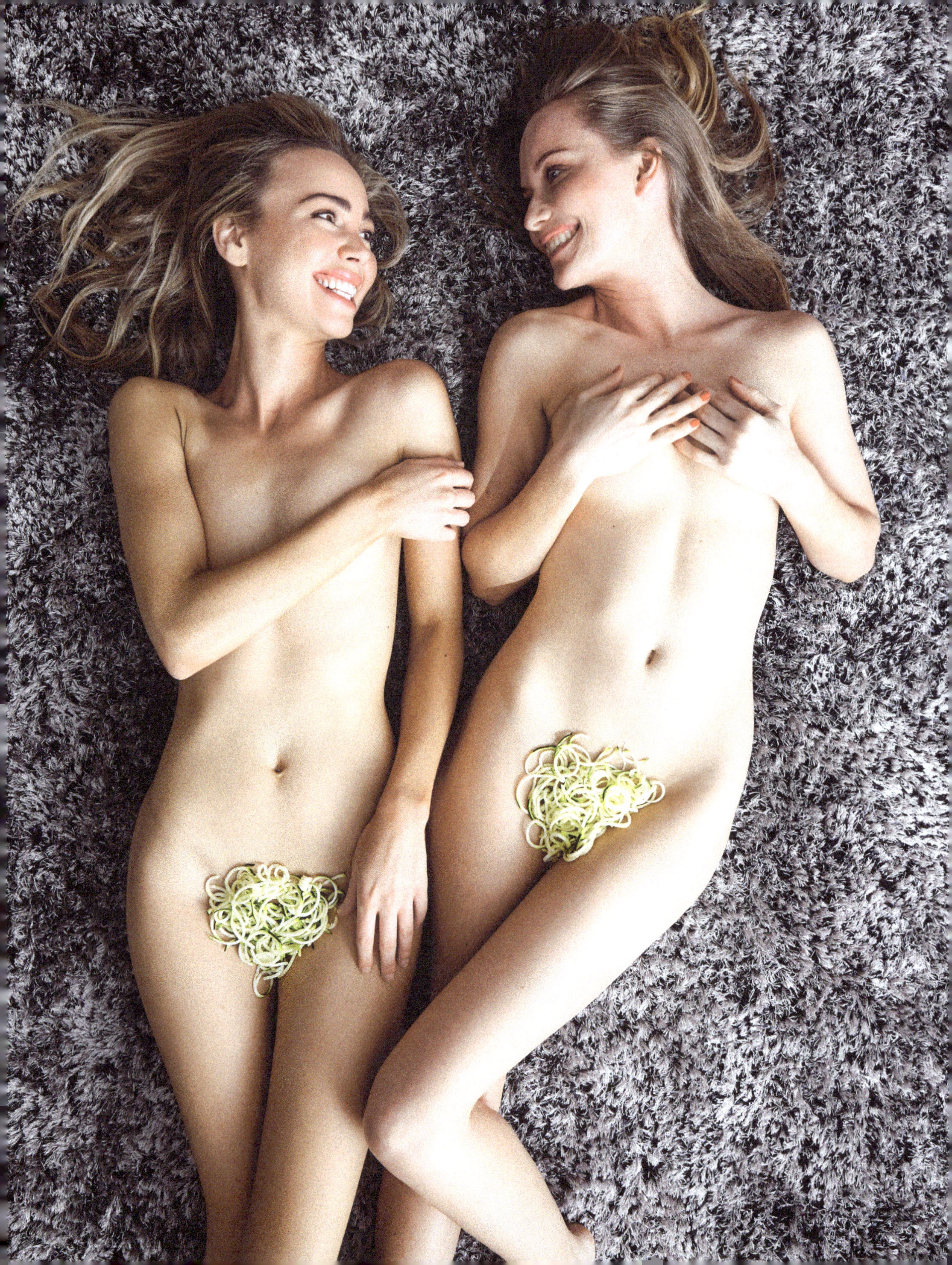

VEGINA

VEGAN BOLOGNAISE WITH ZUCCHINI PASTA

SERVES 4-6

These zucchini spirals are a great healthy alternative to pasta, or even used as underwear. If you're not vegan, add some tinned tuna to the bolognaise to get your meat fix.

3 large field mushrooms
200g tomato passata
¼ cup semi-dried tomatoes
⅓ cup olive oil
1 brown onion, finely chopped
1 small carrot, finely chopped
2 garlic cloves, finely chopped
½ tsp smoked paprika
¼ cup red wine
1 cup tinned brown lentils, drained, rinsed
400g can chopped tomatoes
1 tbs brown sugar
Handful mixed olives, roughly chopped
½ tbs capers, roughly chopped
1 long red chilli, seeded, finely chopped
3 large zucchini
Fresh basil leaves, to serve

CASHEW PARMESAN

½ cup raw cashew nuts
½ tsp salt
1 tsp savoury yeast flakes

1. Preheat oven to 180C. Place mushrooms in a food processor and process until finely chopped. Transfer to a roasting pan and bake for 30 minutes, stirring every 10 minutes. Remove from oven and set aside.

2. Meanwhile, place passata and semi-dried tomatoes in a food processor and process until smooth. Set aside.

3. To make cashew parmesan, place all ingredients into a food processor and process to a fine crumb. Set aside.

4. To make bolognaise, heat oil in a saucepan over medium heat. Add onion, carrot and garlic, and cook for 2 minutes or until softened, then add paprika and red wine, and cook for a further 2 minutes.

5. Add baked mushrooms, passata mixture, lentils, chopped tomatoes, sugar, olives and capers, and season with salt and pepper. Bring to a simmer and cook for 30 minutes or until sauce thickens slightly. Remove from heat and stir through chilli.

6. To make 'zughetti', use a spiraliser to cut zucchini into a spaghetti shape. Alternatively, use a vegetable peeler to create zucchini ribbons, like fettuccini. When ready to serve, place zughetti in a bowl, cover with hot water, and let sit for 20 seconds until tender, then drain.

7. Serve warmed zughetti topped with bolognaise, basil and a sprinkle of cashew parmesan.

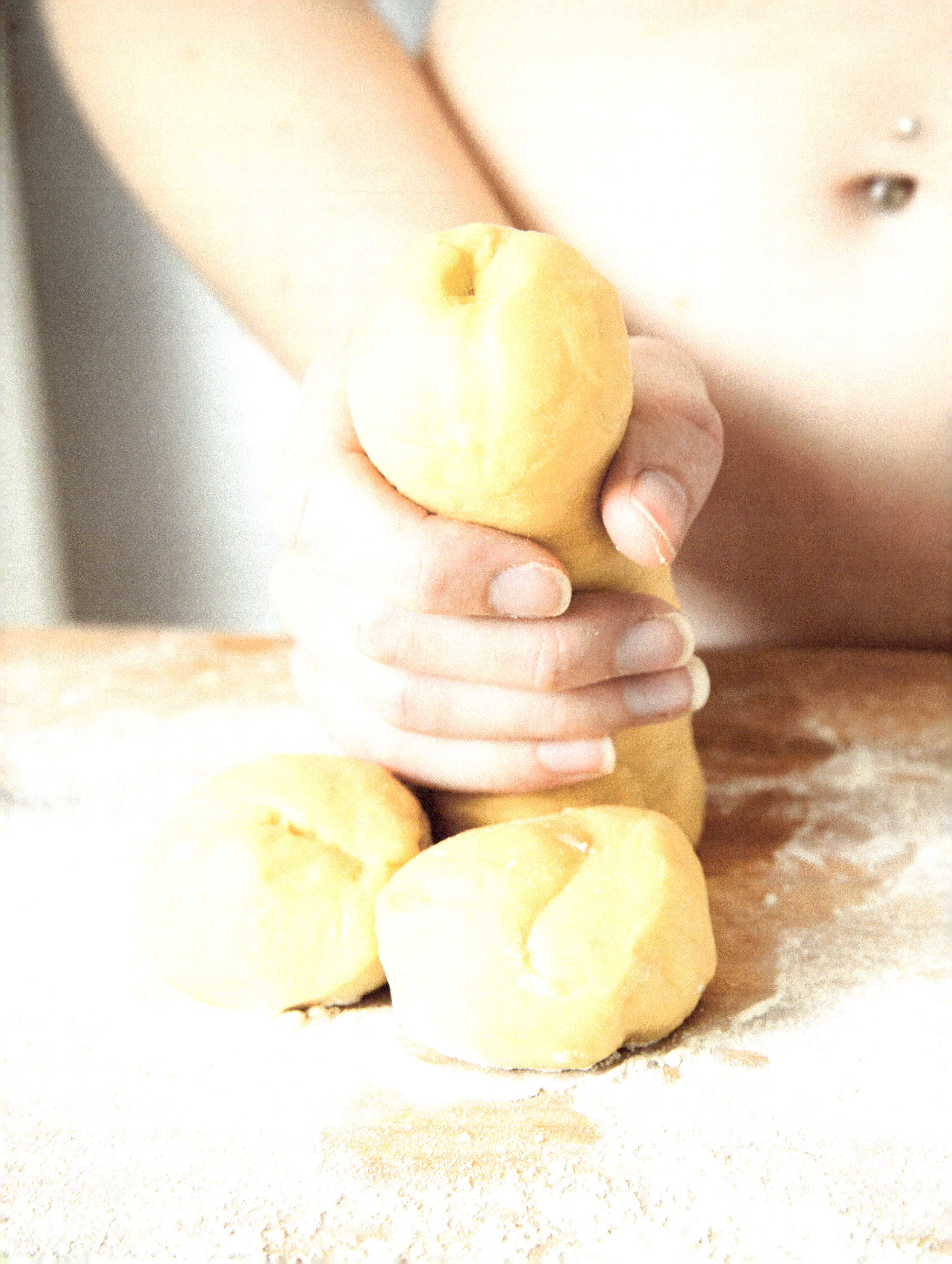

THE HAND JOB

HANDMADE PASTA WITH CHERRY TOMATO SAUCE

This one requires a lot of wrist action. Have fun and get messy in the kitchen with your loved one while preparing this pasta from scratch. A pasta machine will be needed.

SERVES 3-4

200g plain flour
2 extra-large free-range eggs
2 tbs olive oil

3 garlic cloves, finely chopped
1 red onion, finely chopped
¼ cup dry white wine
3 cups cherry tomatoes, halved
Chilli flakes
Fresh basil leaves and grated parmesan, to serve

1. Sift flour and a pinch of salt onto a clean work surface. Make a well in the centre and crack eggs into well. Using your hands, mix flour and eggs together, then knead for 10 minutes or until a soft dough forms. The dough should feel silky and damp but not wet. If the dough is too dry add a little water, if it's too wet add a little extra flour and knead through.

2. Wrap dough in plastic wrap and set aside at room temperature for 10 minutes. Once dough has rested, cut into 3 portions. Using a rolling pin, roll each portion out to a 1cm-thick rectangle, then feed through the largest setting of your pasta machine.

3. Fold rolled pasta sheet in half over itself, then roll out a little with the rolling pin so it fits through the machine again. Feed it back through the highest setting, and repeat this folding and rolling process three more times. This will give your pasta strength and develop great texture. Repeat with remaining dough.

4. Feed each pasta sheet through each setting once until you reach your desired thickness. Lightly dust each pasta sheet with flour.

5. To hand-cut the pasta, gently fold each sheet of pasta over itself a few times and, using a sharp knife, cut pasta to your desired width, then unravel and set aside. Repeat with remaining dough.

6. To make cherry tomato sauce, heat oil in a pan over medium heat, add garlic and onion, and cook for 4 minutes or until softened.

7. Pour in wine and simmer for 2 minutes. Add tomatoes and cook for 4 minutes or until they begin to soften. Stir through chilli flakes and season with a generous pinch of salt

8. Meanwhile, place pasta in salted boiling water and cook for 2-3 minutes or until al dente. Drain and stir through cherry tomato sauce. Serve with fresh basil leaves and grated parmesan.

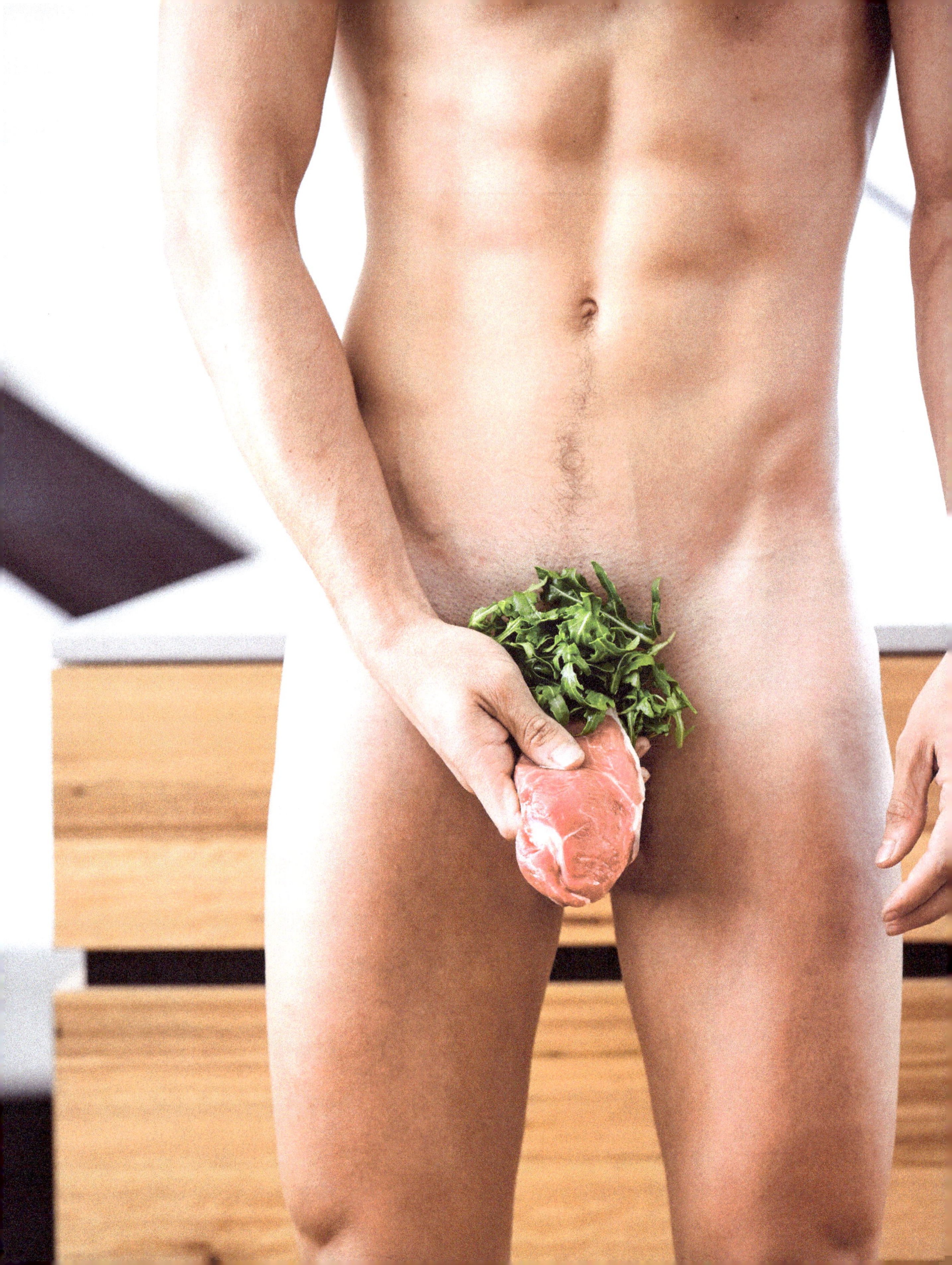

MEATY ROCKET

TAGLIATA

Simple and succulent, this juicy meat will have you salivating. Be sure to use a top-quality steak.

SERVES 2

2 x 250g steaks (I used a dry-aged Wagyu sirloin)
Olive oil, to cook
2 garlic cloves
Two knobs butter
4 thyme sprigs

PARMESAN AND ROCKET SALAD

2 big handfuls baby rocket
2 roma tomatoes, deseeded, finely chopped
¼ cup finely grated parmesan
1 tbs balsamic vinegar
Lemon wedge, juiced

1. Leave steaks covered at room temperature for 1 hour prior to cooking.

2. Heat a pan over high heat. Rub both sides of the steaks with oil and generously season with sea salt.

3. Place steaks in pan and cook to your liking (medium rare works best for this dish). Two-thirds of the way through cooking, bash garlic with the side of a knife so it opens up then add to pan with butter, thyme and a good splash of olive oil. When butter has melted, spoon over steaks continuously until cooked. Remove from heat and place steaks on a board or plate to rest for 5 minutes.

4. Meanwhile, to make salad, place rocket, tomato and parmesan in a bowl, then toss together with balsamic vinegar and lemon juice.

5. Slice steaks into 1cm-thick strips and serve alongside rocket salad. Spoon some of the butter, garlic and thyme sauce from pan over steaks and season with freshly cracked pepper.

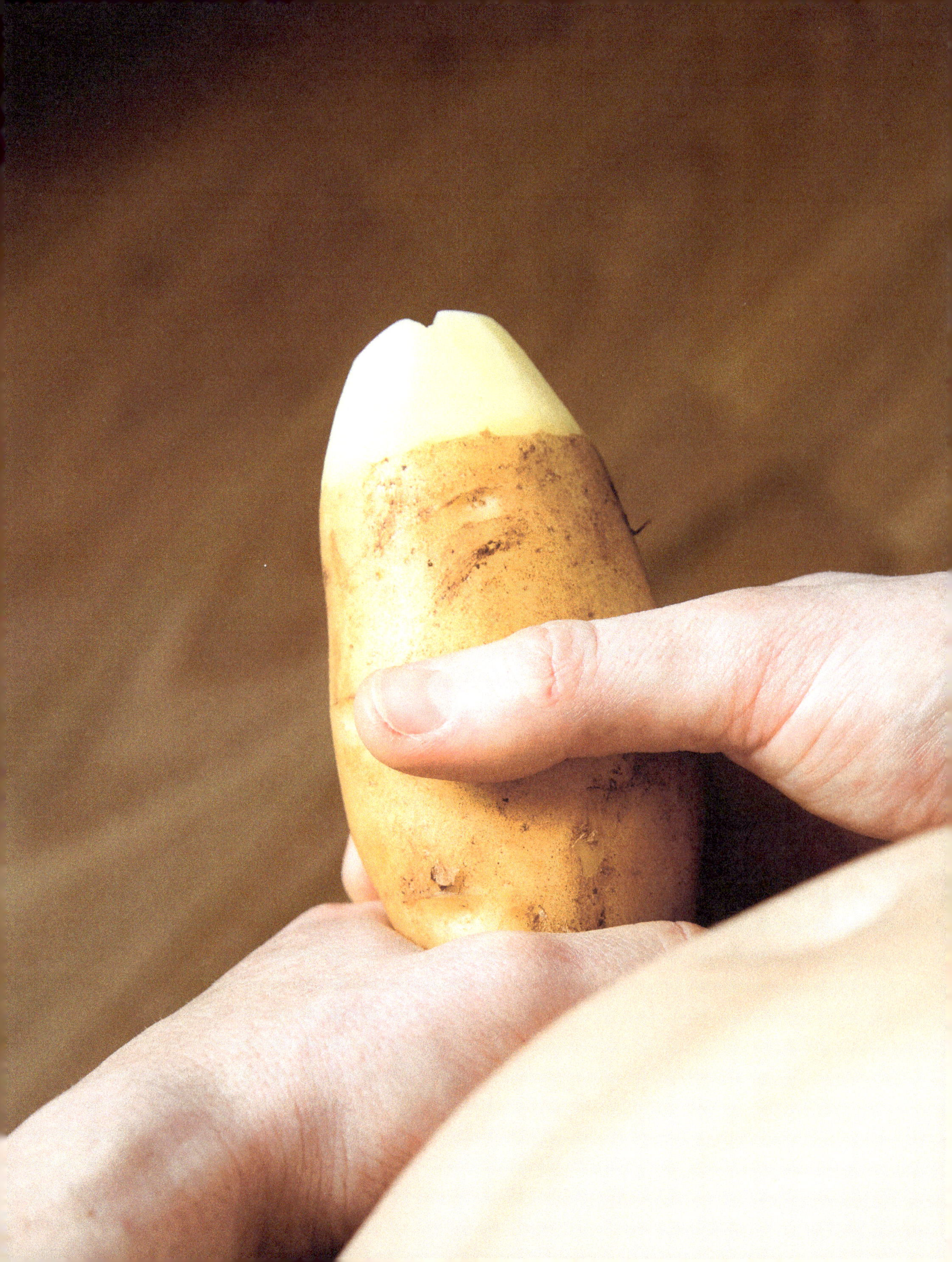

LONG FAT ONES

HAND-CUT WEDGES WITH SPICY TOMATO RELISH

SERVES 4 AS A SNACK OR SIDE DISH

6 roma tomatoes, quartered

2 long red chillies, halved

3 garlic cloves, peeled

½ tsp ground coriander

½ tsp cumin seeds

¼ cup malt vinegar

¼ cup brown sugar

2 tsp sea salt

1 tsp cracked black pepper

Olive oil

2 shallots, finely chopped

Handful fresh tarragon, finely chopped

4 large potatoes suitable for roasting, washed (I used Nicola potatoes)

Dip these long fat members into the delicious spicy relish and swallow a big mouthful of tastiness. Make the relish the day before to develop flavour.

1. To make relish, preheat oven to 150C. Line a large oven tray with baking paper. Place tomato, chilli and garlic into tray. Sprinkle with coriander, cumin salt, and pepper, then drizzle with 2 tbs oil. Place in oven and roast for 1 hour or until tomato is lightly charred and very soft. Set aside to cool for 10 minutes.

2. Place roasted tomato mix into a food processor and blend to a rough sauce. Transfer mixture to a small pan over low heat. Add vinegar and sugar and simmer for 5 minutes, stirring occasionally, or until sugar has dissolved. Remove from heat and stir through shallots and tarragon.

3. Spoon relish into two sterilised 200ml jars and seal. Let jars cool then store in fridge until ready to use. Once opened, use sauce with two weeks. Makes 400ml.

4. To make wedges, preheat oven to 240C. Place potatoes into a large pot of cold water over medium heat. Bring to a gentle simmer, then cook for 15 minutes or until parboiled. Test by inserting a small knife into potatoes, they should be tender but not mushy. Drain potatoes and leave in strainer for 10 minutes or until cool enough to handle. Cut each potato into large fat wedges.

5. Place wedges into a large non-stick roasting pan and drizzle with 3 tbs oil. Bake for 20 minutes or until crunchy and golden brown. Sprinkle with sea salt and serve with tomato relish.

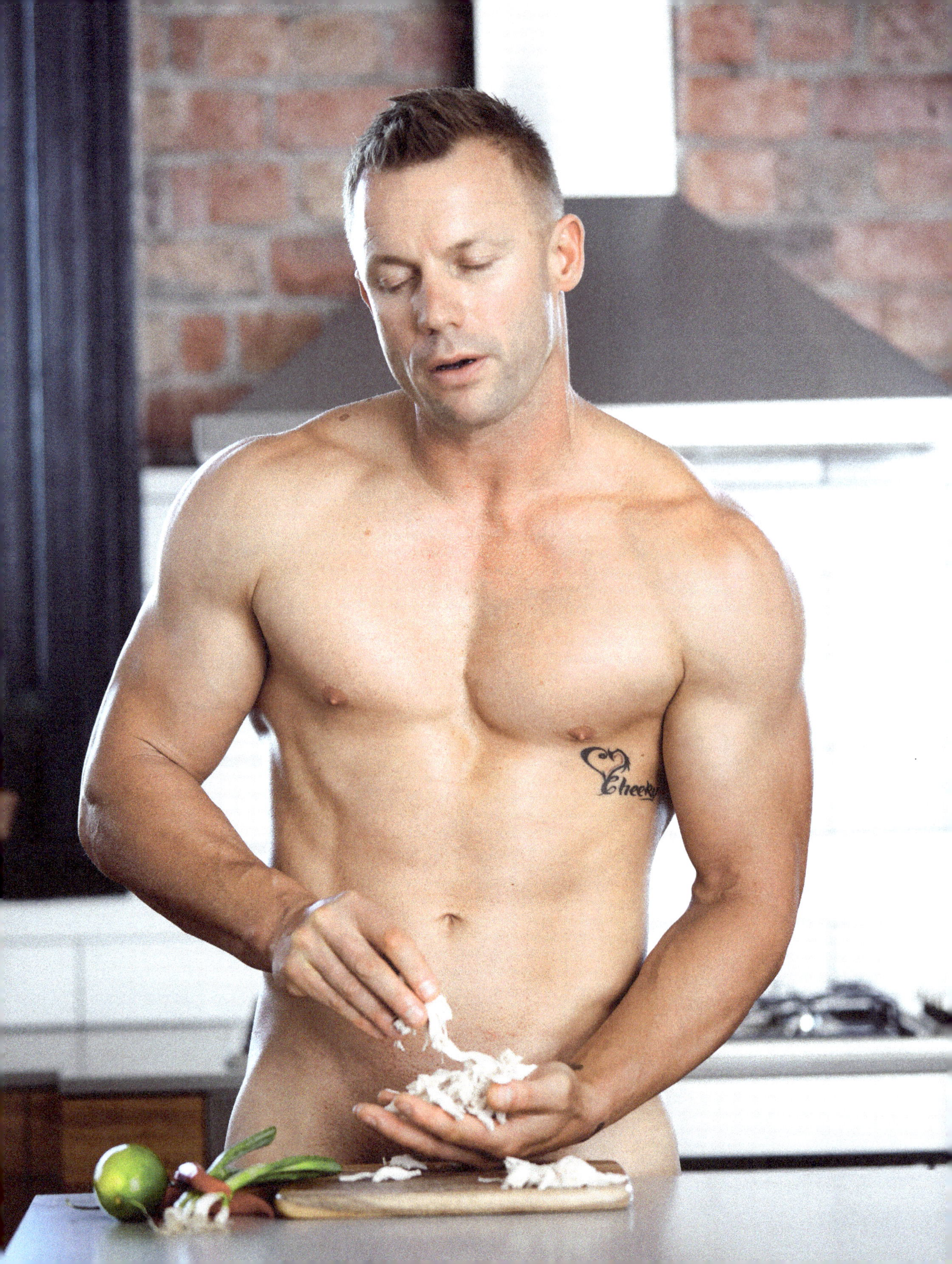
Cheeky

HAVING A PULL
THAI PULLED CHICKEN SALAD

The pulling action in this recipe will result in a beautifully shredded piece of meat. Sex-face optional.

SERVES 4

2 free-range chicken breasts
125g Thai-style rice noodles
1 tsp sesame oil
2 cups shredded wombok
Big handful bean sprouts
2 spring onions, thinly sliced
12 snow peas, thinly sliced
1 Lebanese cucumber, cut into julienne
1 long red chilli, thinly sliced
Big handful torn coriander, mint and Vietnamese mint
Toasted sesame seeds, crushed toasted peanuts and fried shallots, to serve

SALAD DRESSING
1 tbs oyster sauce
1 tbs lime juice
1½ tbs soy sauce
2 tsp honey
1 tsp sesame oil
1 tsp sambal oelek

1. Place chicken in a saucepan, cover with water and bring to a simmer (do not boil). Turn off heat immediately and leave chicken covered in pot for 30 minutes to finishing cooking with residual heat. Remove chicken and shred. Transfer to a bowl, cover and place in fridge to cool.

2. Meanwhile, cook noodles according to packet instructions, drain, rinse with cold water and toss through sesame oil. Set aside.

3. Place wombok, sprouts, onion, snow peas, cucumber, chilli and herbs in a bowl and toss. Combine salad dressing ingredients in a small bowl.

4. To assemble salad, layer noodles, salad, then chicken, with some dressing between each layer. Top with sesame seeds, peanuts and fried shallots.

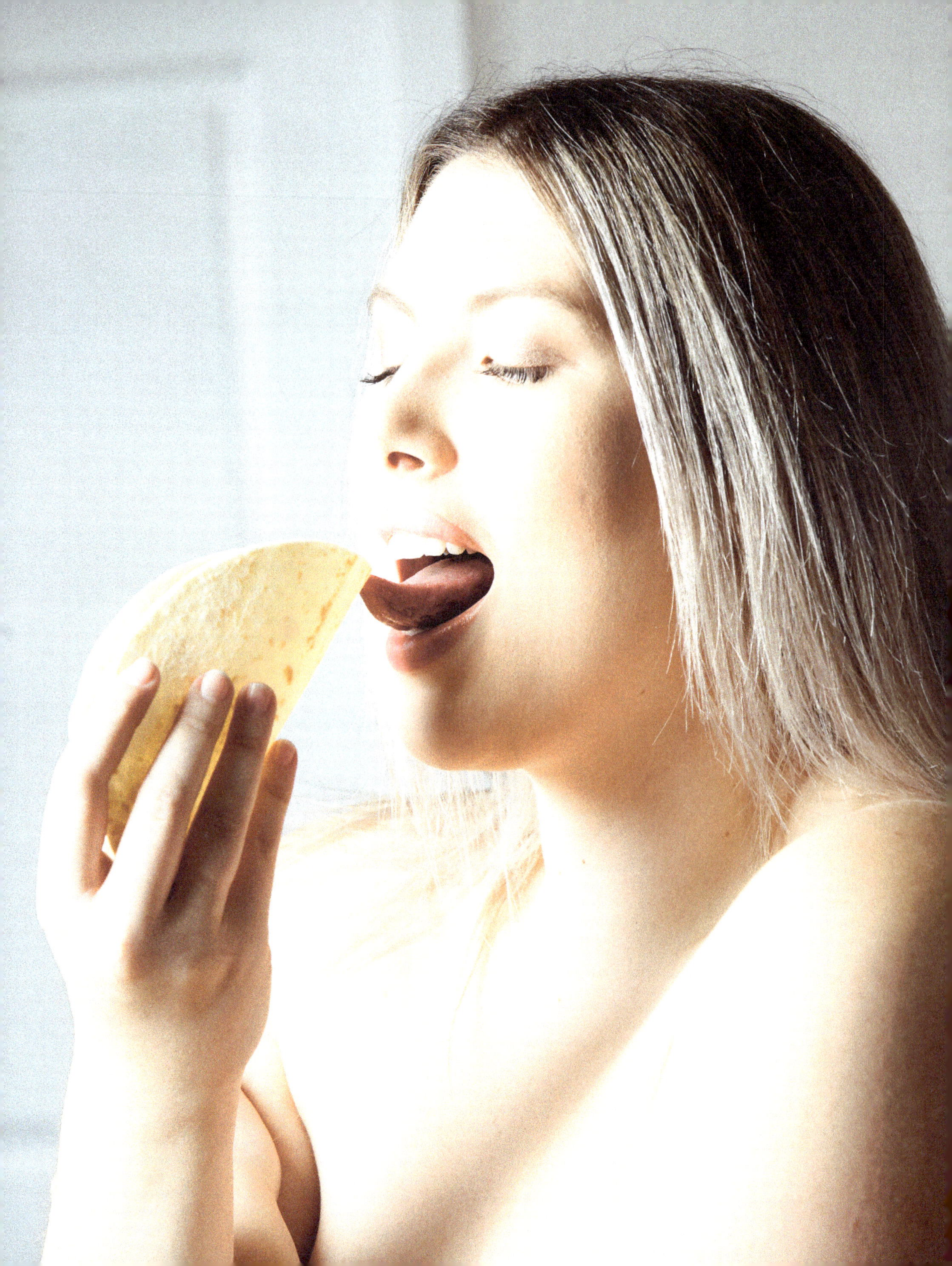

LICK THE TACO

VEGETARIAN TACOS

Spicy mouthfuls for those of you who don't like meat.

SERVES 4

2 tbs olive oil, plus extra, to brush

½ red onion, finely chopped

2 garlic cloves, finely chopped

½ cup tomato passata

3 tomatillos*

2 chipotle peppers in adobo sauce*

1 tbs soy sauce

1 tsp brown sugar

1 tsp smoked paprika

3 large corn cobs

400g can black beans drained, rinsed

12 small corn tortillas

Crumbled fetta and lime wedges, to serve

SLAW

½ savoy cabbage, finely shredded

Bunch fresh coriander, roughly chopped

4 spring onions, thinly sliced

1 long red chilli, finely chopped

1 lime, juiced

1. To make taco sauce, heat oil in a pan over medium heat, add onion and garlic and cook for 4 minutes or until softened and lightly caramelised. Transfer to a food processor or blender with passata, tomatillos, peppers, soy sauce, sugar and paprika and process until smooth. Set aside.

2. To make slaw, combine all ingredients in a bowl and toss to combine. Set aside.

3. Brush corn with oil then grill until cooked all over and slightly charred. Set aside to cool for 5 minutes then shave corn kernels off cobs and place in a pot over low-medium heat with black beans and taco sauce until heated through.

4. Meanwhile, heat each tortilla in a lightly oiled pan over a high heat (20-30sec each side). Wrap in a clean, damp dishtowel to keep them warm as you go.

5. To serve, top each warmed tortilla with taco sauce mix, slaw, crumbled fetta and a lime wedge on the side.

*Tomatillos and chipotle peppers in adobo sauce are available from select greengrocers and Mexican food shops.

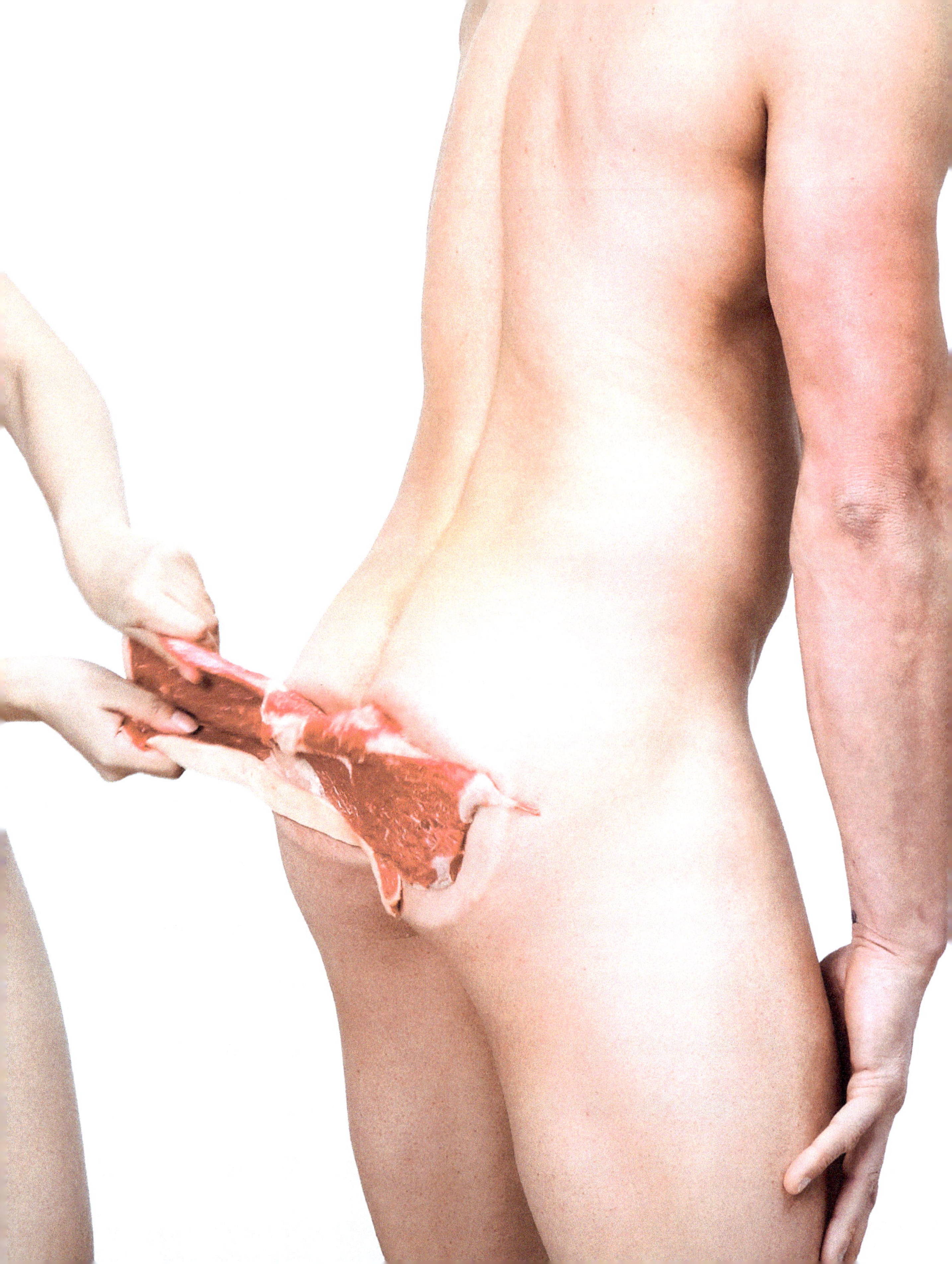

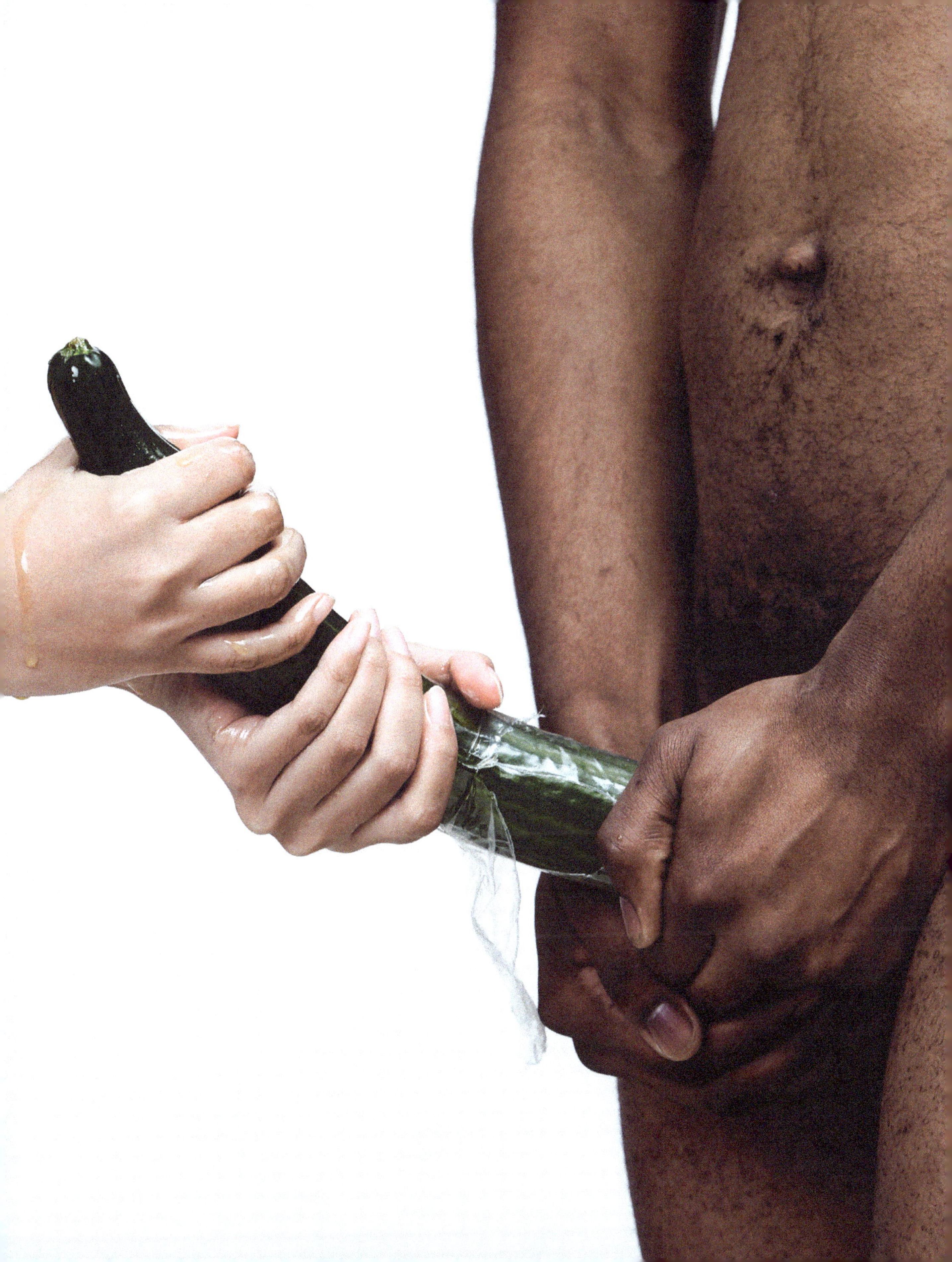

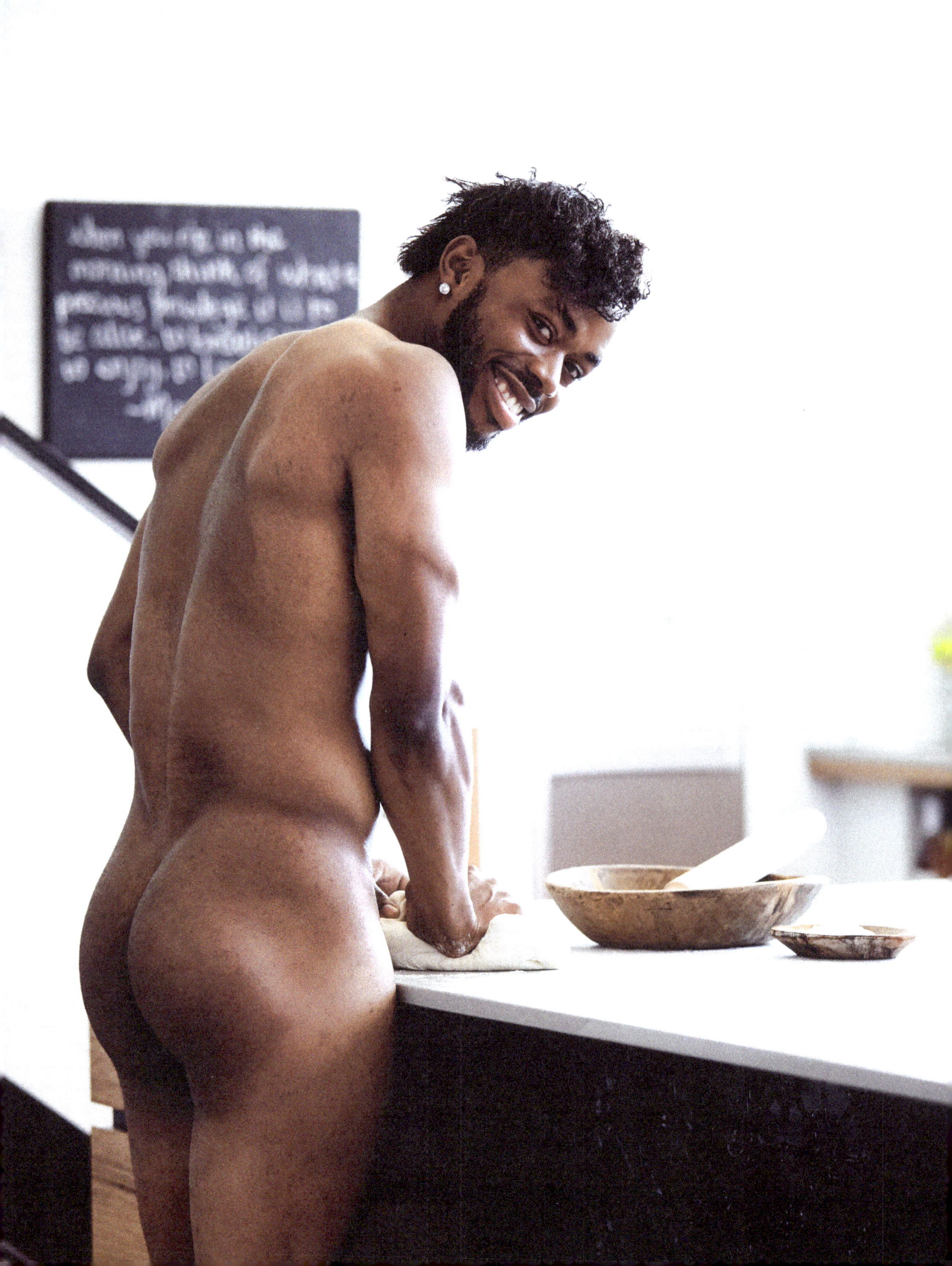

YOU KNEAD IT

HOMEMADE PIZZA

*You know you want this. Grip with both hands and massage vigorously while preparing the dough.
Use whatever toppings you like. As a rule of thumb, use no more than three ingredients, something cheesey, something salty and something fresh.*

MAKES 6-8 MEDIUM PIZZAS

2 x 7g packets dried yeast
650ml lukewarm water
2 tsp raw sugar
⅓ cup olive oil
1kg plain flour, plus extra, to dust
2 tsp sea salt
Pizza toppings of your choice, to serve

PIZZA BASE SAUCE
1kg overripe roma tomatoes, halved
1 garlic clove, chopped
2 tbs olive oil
1 tsp sea salt

1. Preheat oven to 140C. To make pizza base sauce, place tomatoes skin-side down on an oven tray, top with garlic, drizzle over oil and season with salt.

2. Cover with foil, making a few small holes for steam to escape, then bake in oven for 3 hours. Remove foil and bake for a further 20 minutes or until lightly caramelised. Remove from oven, and set aside to cool for 10 minutes.

3. Poor off excess water and oil, then place tomatoes in a food processor and process to a chunky sauce consistency.

4. To make pizza dough, dissolve yeast in water in a large bowl. Stir in sugar and oil and set aside in a warm place for 10 minutes to activate yeast. Sift flour into a large bowl then add salt and yeast mixture.

5. Using your hands, mix ingredients until a dough starts to form. Transfer onto a work surface lightly dusted with flour and continue to knead for a further 5 minutes.

6. Place dough in a greased bowl and cover with a damp tea towel. Set aside in a warm, draught-free place for 1 hour or until dough doubles in size.

7. Preheat oven to 240C. Turn dough out onto bench and knock out the air with a fist. Cut into 6 pieces then roll out pizza bases, dusting bench with flour for each. Wrap any left over portions in plastic wrap and freeze for another day.

8. Working in batches, place each base on an oiled pizza tray, top with sauce and your favourite toppings, and bake for 15 minutes or until cooked.

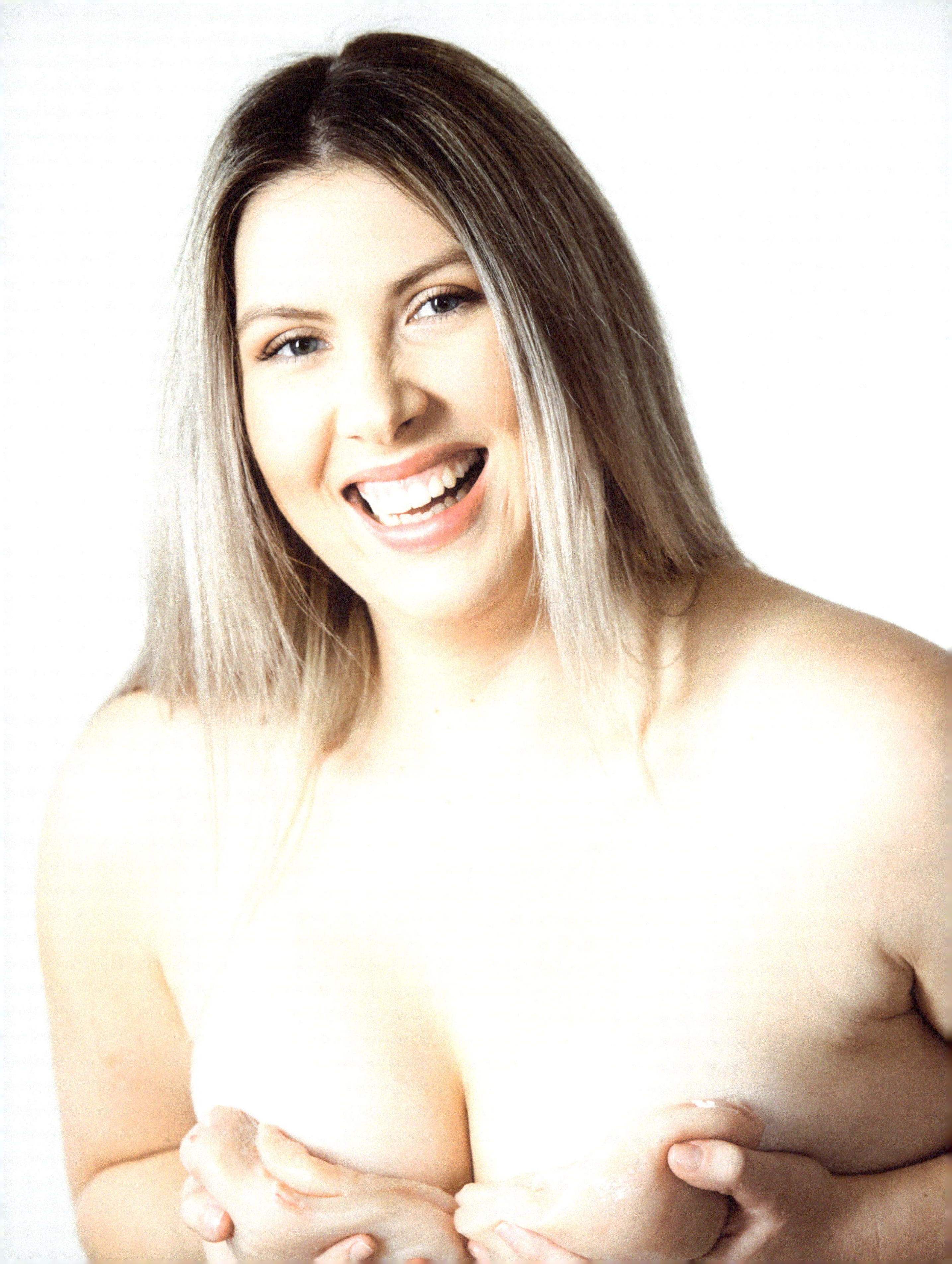

JUICY BREASTS

CHICKEN PARMIGIANA

These juicy chicken tits are perfectly paired with some roast vegetables and a simple salad.

SERVES 4

4 slices day-old white bread, roughly chopped
1 garlic clove, roughly chopped
Handful fresh parsley, roughly chopped
½ lemon, zested
2 free-range chicken breasts
½ cup plain flour
2 free-range eggs, beaten
Olive oil, to shallow-fry
400g chunky tomato passata
1 cup grated mozzarella
2 thyme sprigs, leaves picked
½ cup finely grated parmesan
Cracked black pepper to serve

1. Place bread, garlic, parsley and lemon zest into a food processor and process to a coarse crumb. Set aside.

2. Butterfly each chicken breast and flatten using a meat mallet. Cut each breast into two pieces.

3. Place flour, eggs and breadcrumbs in separate shallow bowls. Dust chicken with flour, shake off excess, then dip in egg and coat in breadcrumbs. Repeat for each fillet. Set aside.

4. Heat oil in a high-sided frying pan over medium-high heat. Add crumbed fillets and cook for 3 minutes each side, or until golden brown and just cooked through. Drain on absorbent paper, then place side-by-side in a roasting pan.

5. Top chicken with passata, mozzarella, thyme and parmesan. Place under a grill and cook until cheese is melted and golden. Set aside to cool for 5 minutes. Season with cracked black pepper and serve.

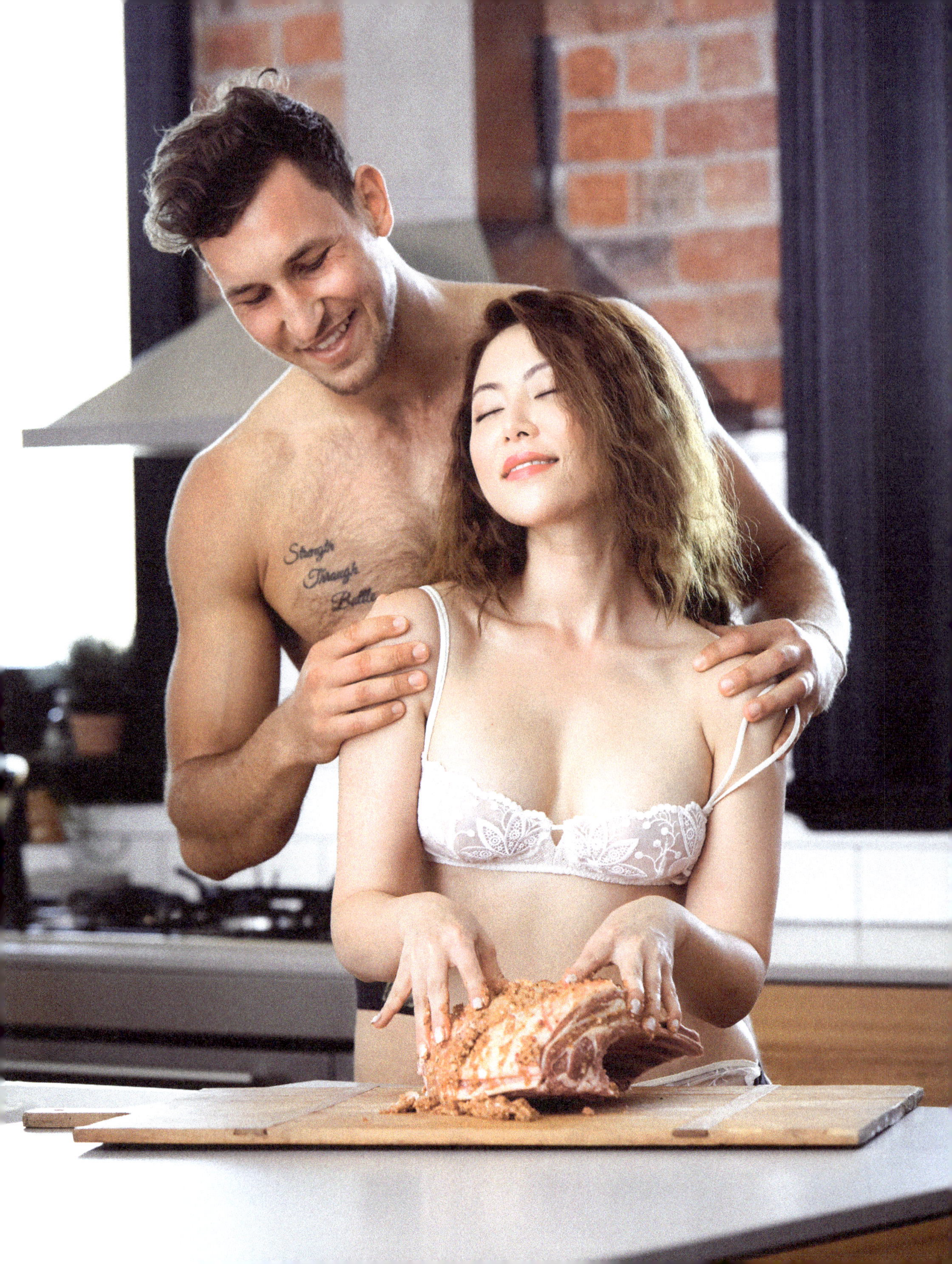

SHOULDER RUB

SLOW-ROASTED LAMB SHOULDER WITH TZATZIKI

SERVES 8

1 large red onion, chopped
4 garlic cloves
1 tbs dried oregano
2 tsp sweet paprika
1 tsp cracked black pepper
2 tsp sea salt
1 lemon, juiced
2 tbs red wine vinegar
⅓ cup olive oil
1 tbs honey
2-2.5kg bone-in lamb shoulder, excess fat trimmed

Lemon wedges, and seasonal sides of your choice, to serve

TZATZIKI
1 cup Greek yoghurt
1 Lebanese cucumber, grated, juice squeezed out
Handful fresh dill, chopped
½ lemon, juiced
½ tsp finely grated garlic
1 tsp salt
4 tbs extra virgin olive oil

The perfect dish for a big feast... or key party. The massage action will help the flavours penetrate deeper into the meat. Start this recipe a day ahead.

1. To make marinade, place onion, garlic, herbs and spices, lemon juice, vinegar, oil and honey in a food processor and process to a coarse paste.

2. Coat lamb shoulder all over with marinade paste, then seal in an airtight container and refrigerate overnight to allow flavours to develop. Remove from fridge 1 hour before cooking.

3. To make tzatziki, combine all ingredients in a bowl, cover and refrigerate overnight.

4. When ready to cook, preheat oven to 140C. Wrap lamb shoulder in baking paper then wrap and seal with foil, place in a heavy-based roasting pan and roast for 4 hours or until meat is tender and falling off the bone.

5. Remove baking paper and foil, return lamb to roasting pan, increase oven to 220C, and roast for a further 15-20 minutes or until lamb starts to caramelise. Remove from oven and set aside to rest for 10 minutes.

6. Using a fork, shred meat and serve with tzatziki, lemon wedges and a selection of your favourite sides.

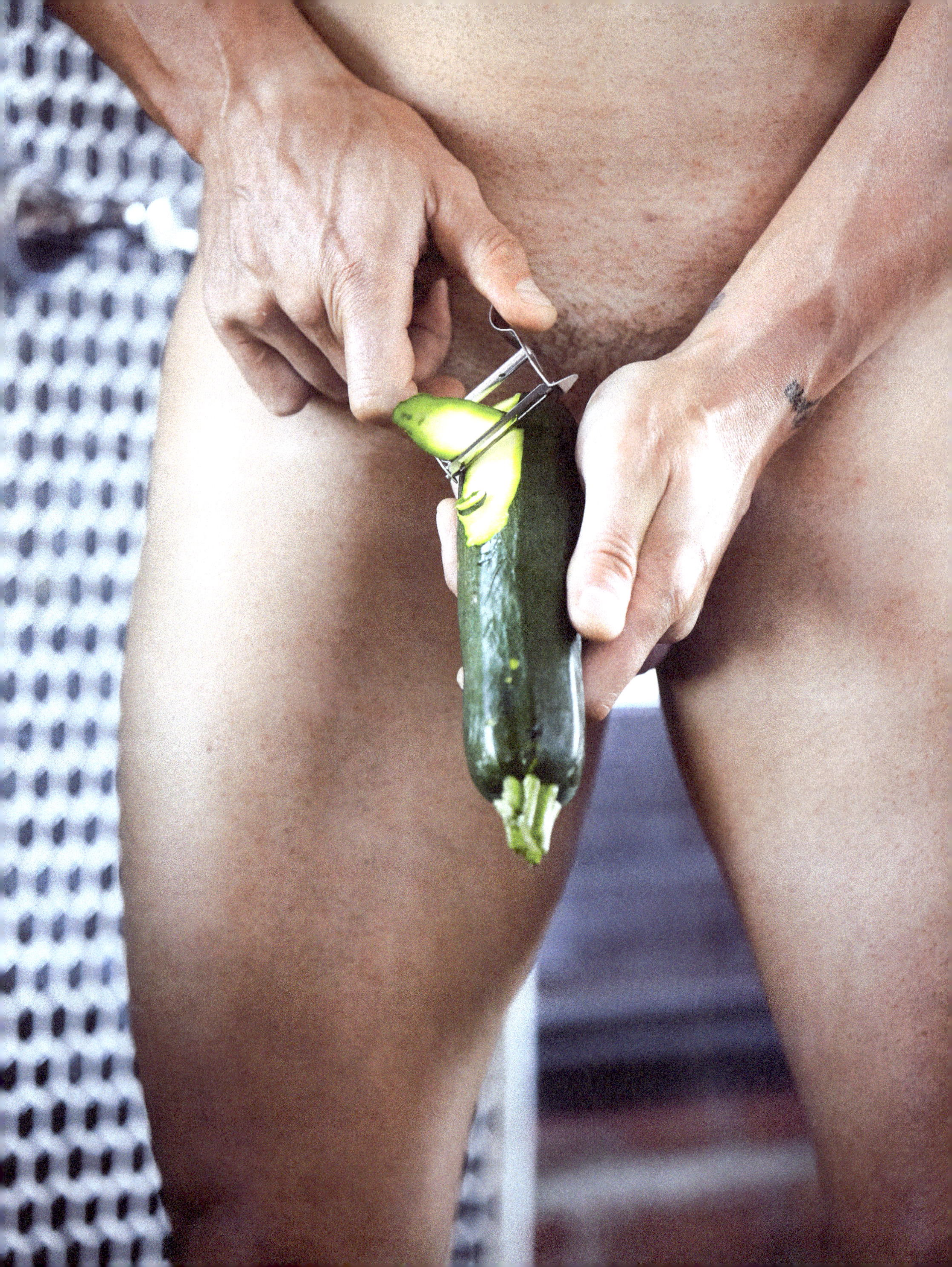

SHAVED
GRILLED ZUCCHINI AND FREEKEH SALAD

The shaved ingredients in this salad provide a clean crisp mouth feel. Great as a side or enjoyed as a light meal on its own.

SERVES 6 AS A SIDE

1 cup freekeh (roasted green wheat grains)

1 large zucchini, shaved into long strips

1 small fennel bulb, finely shaved, tossed in a little lemon juice to prevent browning

4 radishes, finely shaved

2 handfuls rocket

50g shaved parmesan

¼ cup pine nuts, toasted

3 tbs olive oil

1 tbs red wine vinegar

1 tsp raw sugar

Salt and pepper

1. Place freekeh in a pot of cold water over medium heat. Bring to a simmer, then reduce heat to low, cover and cook for 40 minutes or until al dente. Drain and set aside.

2. Heat a griddle pan over high heat. Working in batches, grill zucchini for 1 minute each side or until slightly charred. Set aside.

3. Combine oil, vinegar and sugar in a small bowl, season with salt and pepper, and stir until sugar dissolves. Place freekeh in a serving bowl with remaining salad ingredients. Toss with dressing and serve.

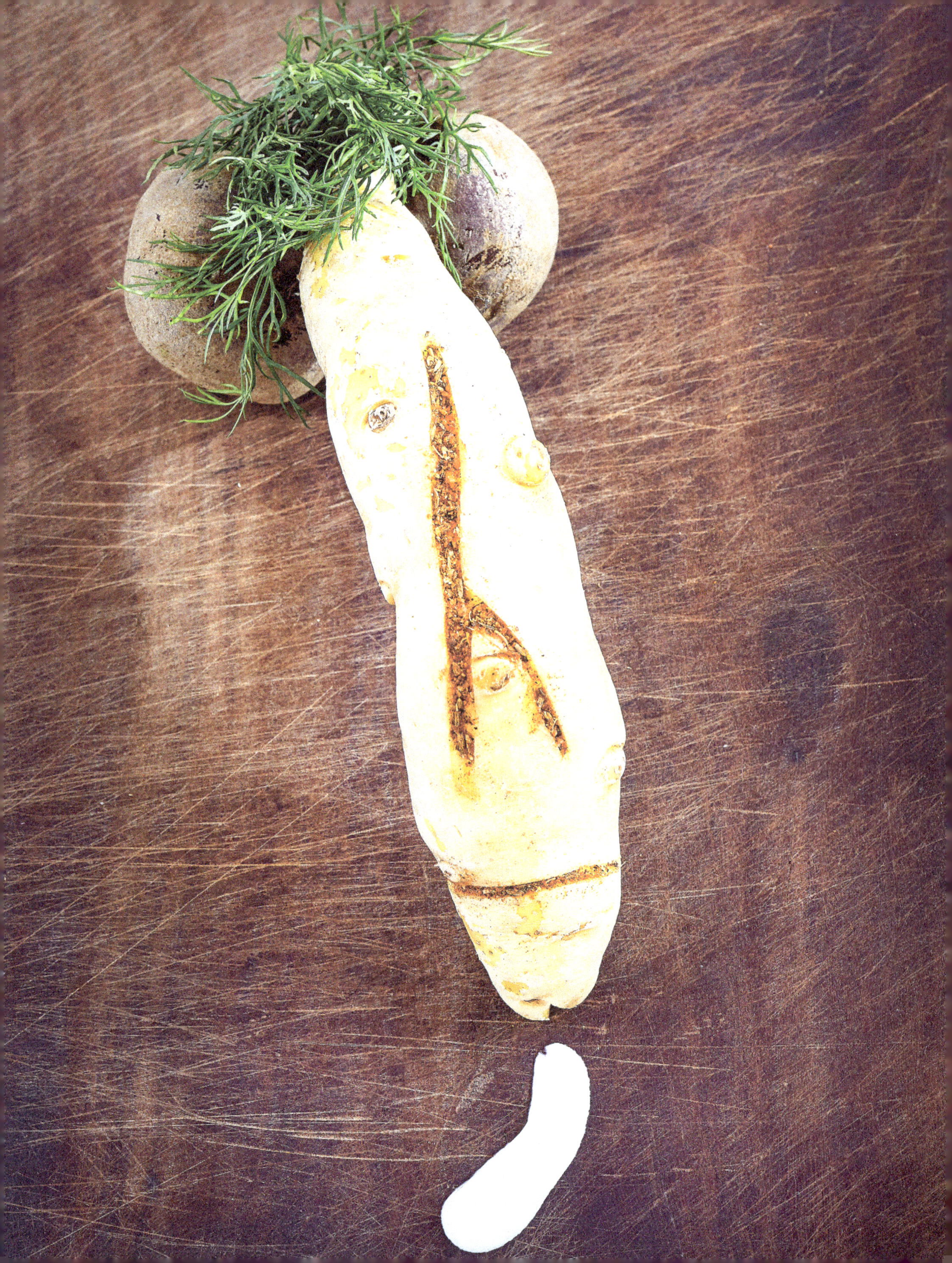

SPICY ROOT

CAJUN SPICED ROAST VEGETABLE SALAD

Experience a good old-fashioned rooting with this spicy side salad, a great addition to some grilled salmon or a Sunday roast.

SERVES 6 AS A SIDE

4 small beetroot

1 red onion, cut into wedges

4 kipfler potatoes, cut into quarters

1 cup butternut pumpkin, cut into large chunks

4 garlic cloves, skin on, halved

3 tbs olive oil

4 cubes goat's fetta, crumbled

Handful hazelnuts, toasted, lightly crushed

Handful pepitas, toasted

Handful fresh parsley sprigs

CAJUN SPICE MIX

½ tsp coriander seeds

½ tsp fennel seeds

1 tsp dried oregano

1 tsp sea salt

1 tsp cracked black pepper

1 tsp paprika

¼ tsp chilli powder, optional

½ tsp smoked paprika

DILL YOGHURT

¼ cup Greek yoghurt

Handful fresh dill, chopped

½ lemon, juiced

1. Preheat oven to 180C. Wrap each beetroot in foil with a pinch of salt, and bake for 45 minutes or until tender when tested with a skewer. Cut into wedges and set aside.

2. Using a mortar and pestle, grind coriander, fennel seeds and oregano to a rough powder, then mix in remaining spices.

3. Toss onion, potato, pumpkin and garlic in spice mix and olive oil. Place in a large roasting pan and bake for 25 minutes, turning after 15 minutes, or until tender. Remove from oven and set aside.

4. Meanwhile, to make dill yoghurt, combine all ingredients in a bowl and season with salt.

5. Arrange vegetables on a large platter, top with crumbled goat's cheese, hazelnuts, pepitas and parsley and drizzle with yoghurt, to serve.

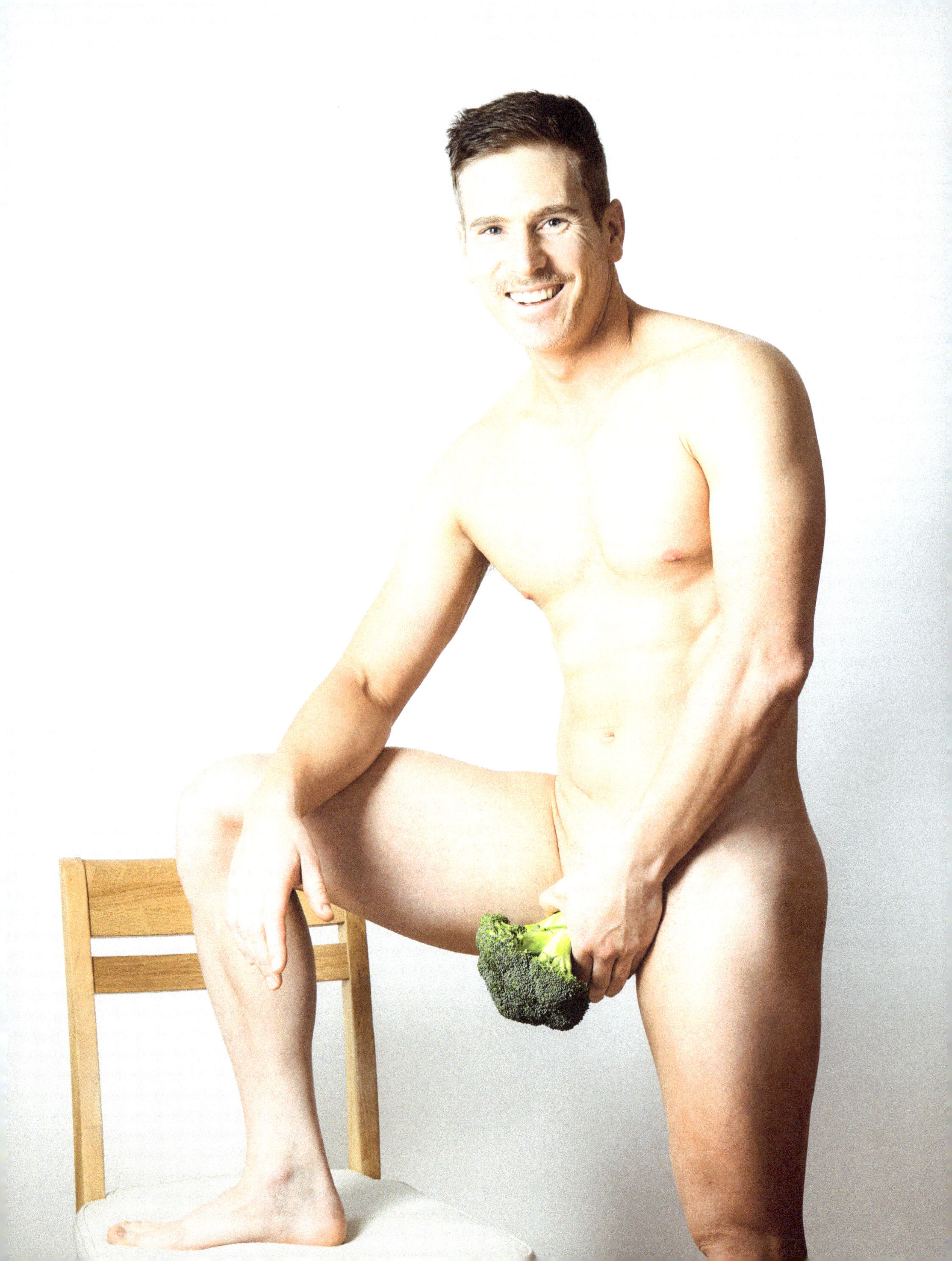

GET YOUR BROC OUT

CHARRED BROCCOLI SALAD

Everyone loves a bit of broccoli head, but the stem also adds a beautiful nutty flavour to this dish, so don't discard it.

SERVES 4 AS A SIDE DISH

1 thick slice sourdough, roughly chopped

1 garlic clove, peeled

½ lemon, zested, juiced

3 tbs olive oil

Large broccoli, cut into florets, stem trimmed and cut into matchsticks

1 cup fresh peas

Handful fresh mint leaves

¼ cup almonds, toasted, roughly chopped

¼ cup grated pecorino cheese

Salt and pepper

1. Preheat oven to 250C. Place bread, garlic, lemon zest and a pinch of salt into a food processor and process to a chunky crumb. Heat 1 tbs olive oil in a pan over medium heat. Add crumb mixture and cook for 5 minutes, stirring occasionally, or until breadcrumbs are golden and crunchy. Remove from heat and set aside in a small bowl.

2. Place broccoli florets and stem into a large roasting pan lined with baking paper. Drizzle with remaining 2 tbs oil and season with salt and pepper. Place in oven and roast for 10 minutes or until florets and stems are lightly charred. Transfer to a large salad bowl.

3. Meanwhile, blanch peas in boiling water for 90 seconds, then drain and add to broccoli. Set aside to cool slightly before adding remaining ingredients.

4. Add mint, almonds, pecorino and lemon juice to broccoli and peas, and toss until combined. Serve salad topped with toasted breadcrumbs.

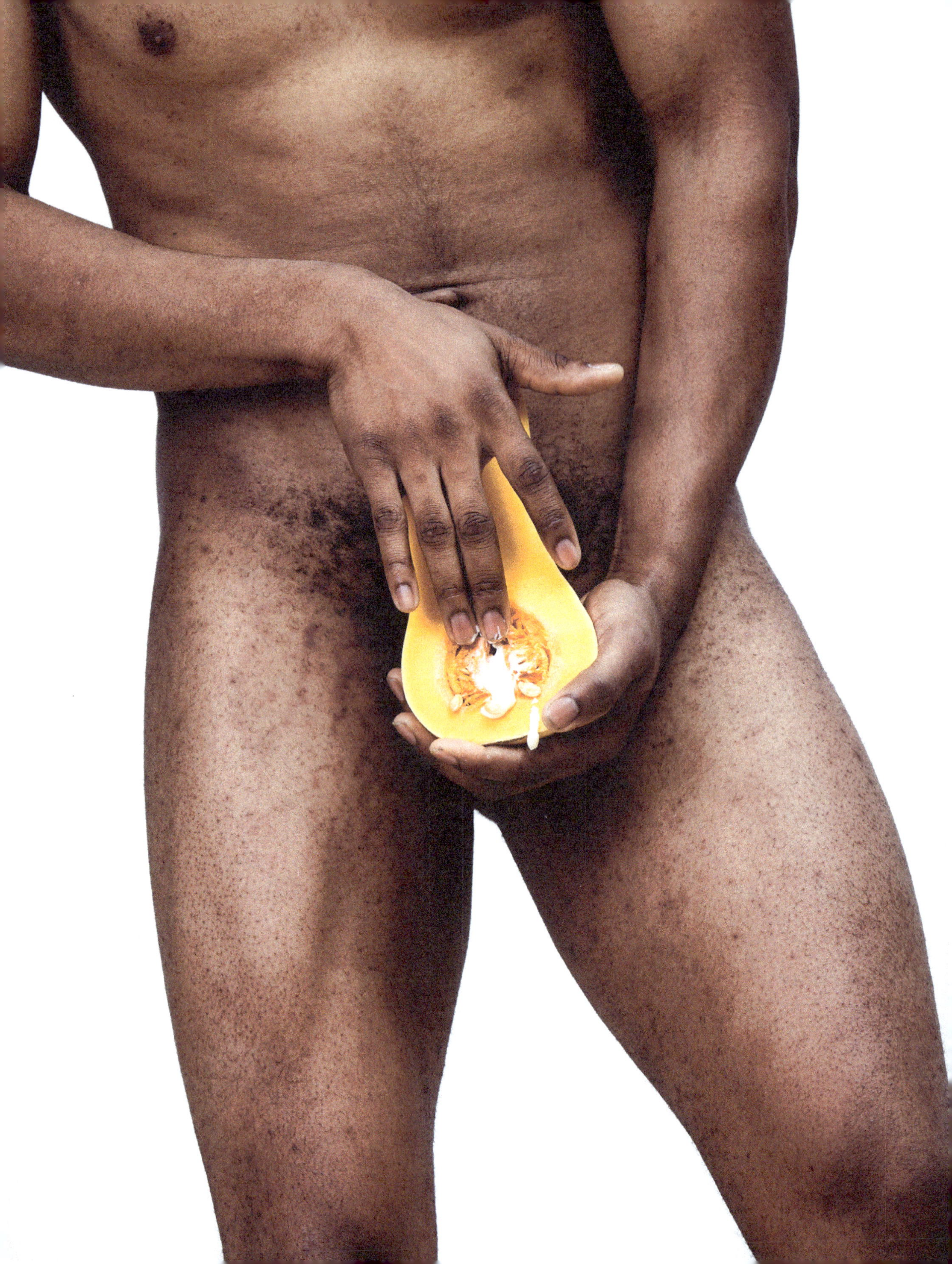

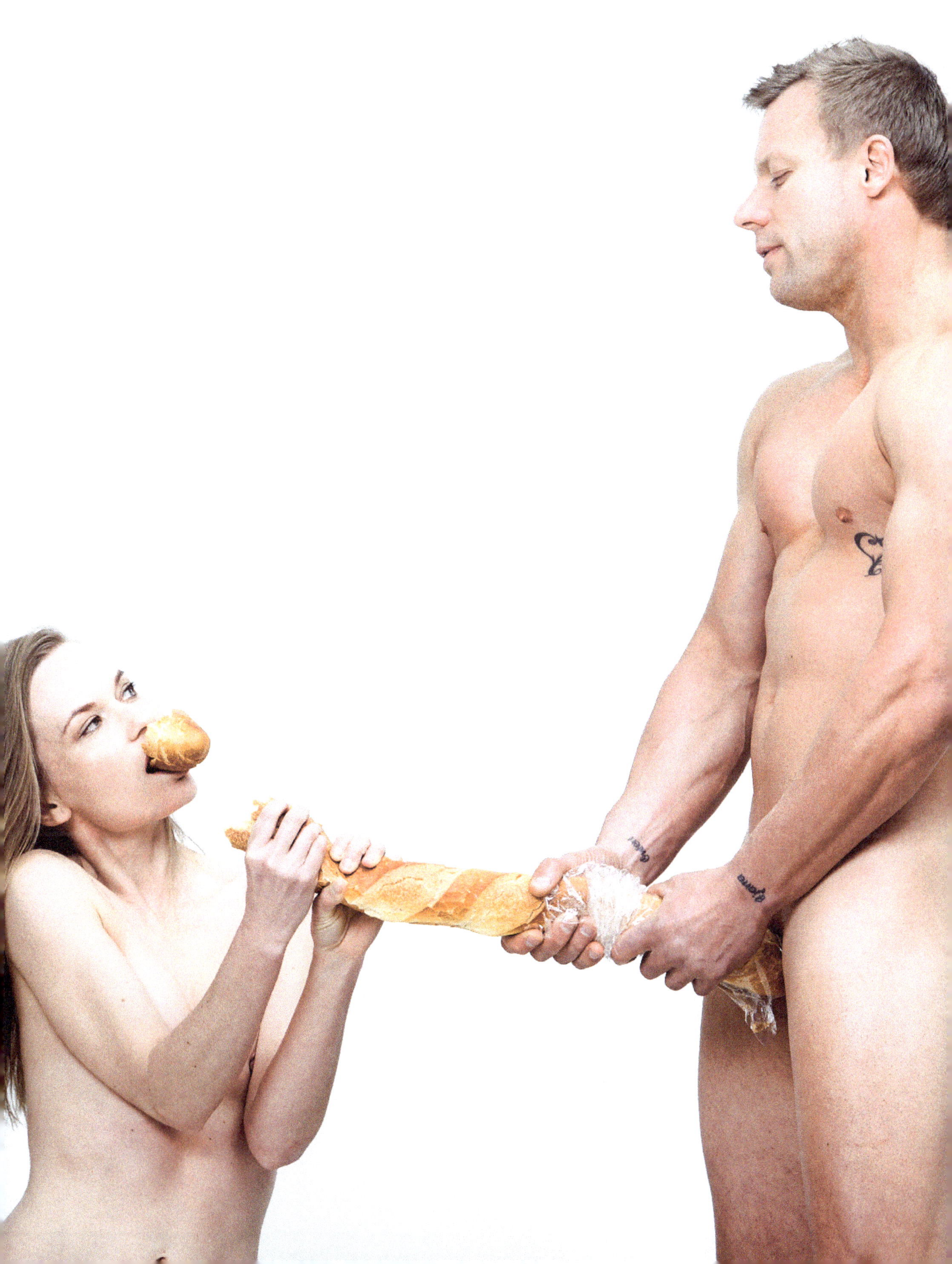

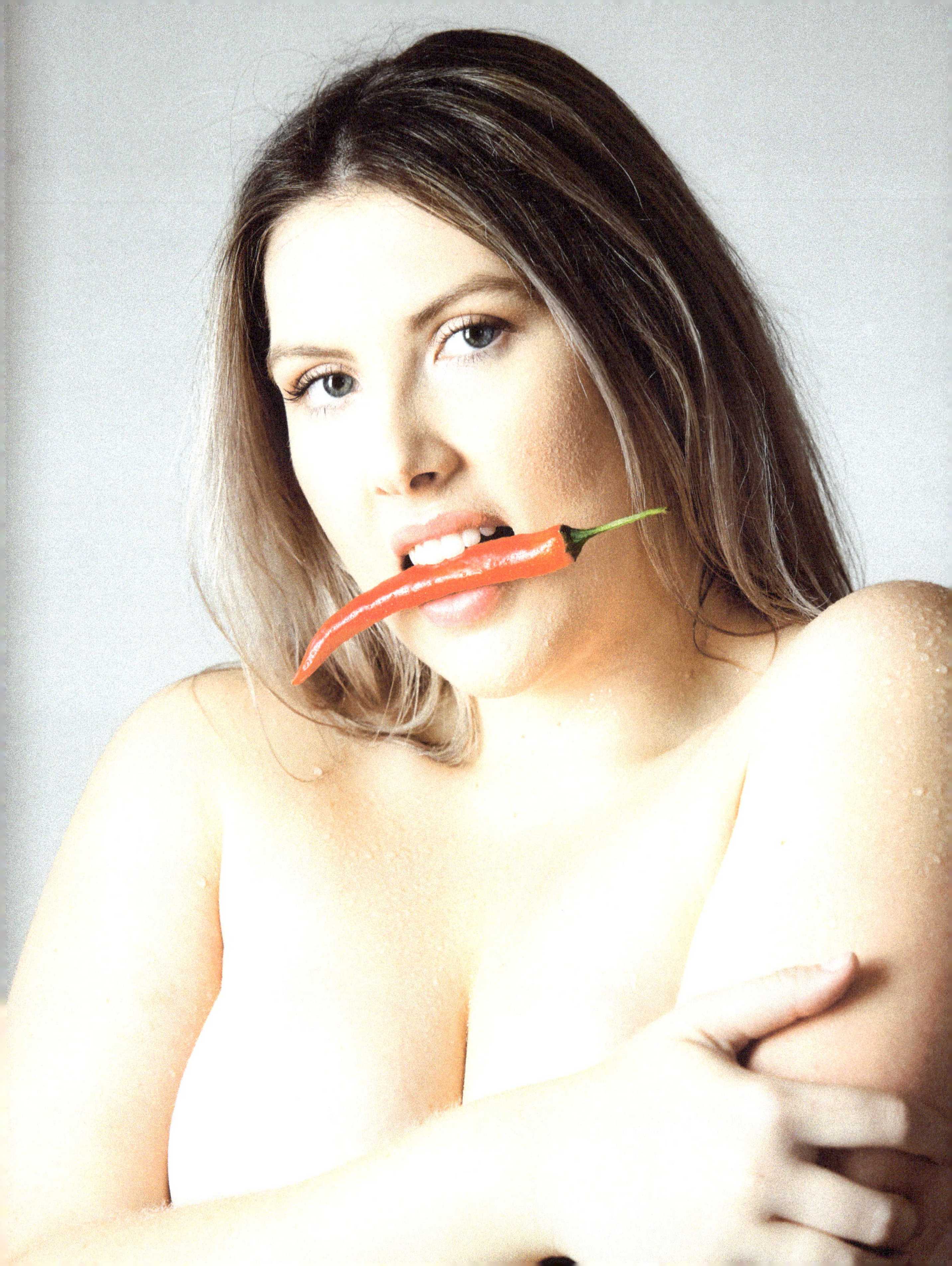

MAKE ME SWEAT

SPICY BEEF CHEEK CURRY

SERVES 4

1kg beef cheeks, trimmed, cut into large chunks (alternatively, use stewing beef)

1 tbs tamarind paste

1 tsp chilli powder (½ tsp for less heat)

1 tsp ground cumin

1 tsp garam masala

1 tsp ground turmeric

2 tsp sea salt

1 tsp cracked black pepper

1 cup Greek yoghurt

Handful fresh mint, roughly chopped

Vegetable oil, to cook

1 tsp brown mustard seeds

1 tsp fenugreek seeds

Thumb-size piece ginger, finely grated

3 garlic cloves, finely grated

2 onions, finely chopped

8 fresh curry leaves

400g tin chopped tomatoes

1 cinnamon stick

Steamed basmati rice and pappadums to serve

This spice-filled dish will leave you feeling hot, sweaty and deeply satisfied. Add some root veg during the roasting phase for a more wholesome meal – just be sure to add extra water so the curry doesn't dry out.

1. Toss beef with tamarind, chilli, cumin, garam masala, turmeric, salt and pepper, cover and set aside in the fridge to marinate for at least 30 minutes, overnight is preferred.

2. Preheat oven to 120C. Combine yoghurt and mint and set aside in fridge.

3. Heat a large heavy-based ovenproof casserole dish over low-medium heat. Pour in enough oil to cover base of pot. Add mustard and fenugreek seeds and cook for 30 seconds or until fenugreek starts to brown slightly.

   Add ginger and garlic and cook for a further minute. Add onion and curry leaves and cook for 5 minutes or until onion has softened and is lightly caramelised. Add beef and cook until browned all over. Stir through tomatoes, ½ cup water and cinnamon stick.

4. Cover with lid, place in oven and cook for 3-4 hours or until beef is very tender and falls apart.

5. Serve curry with steamed basmati rice, pappadums and mint yoghurt.

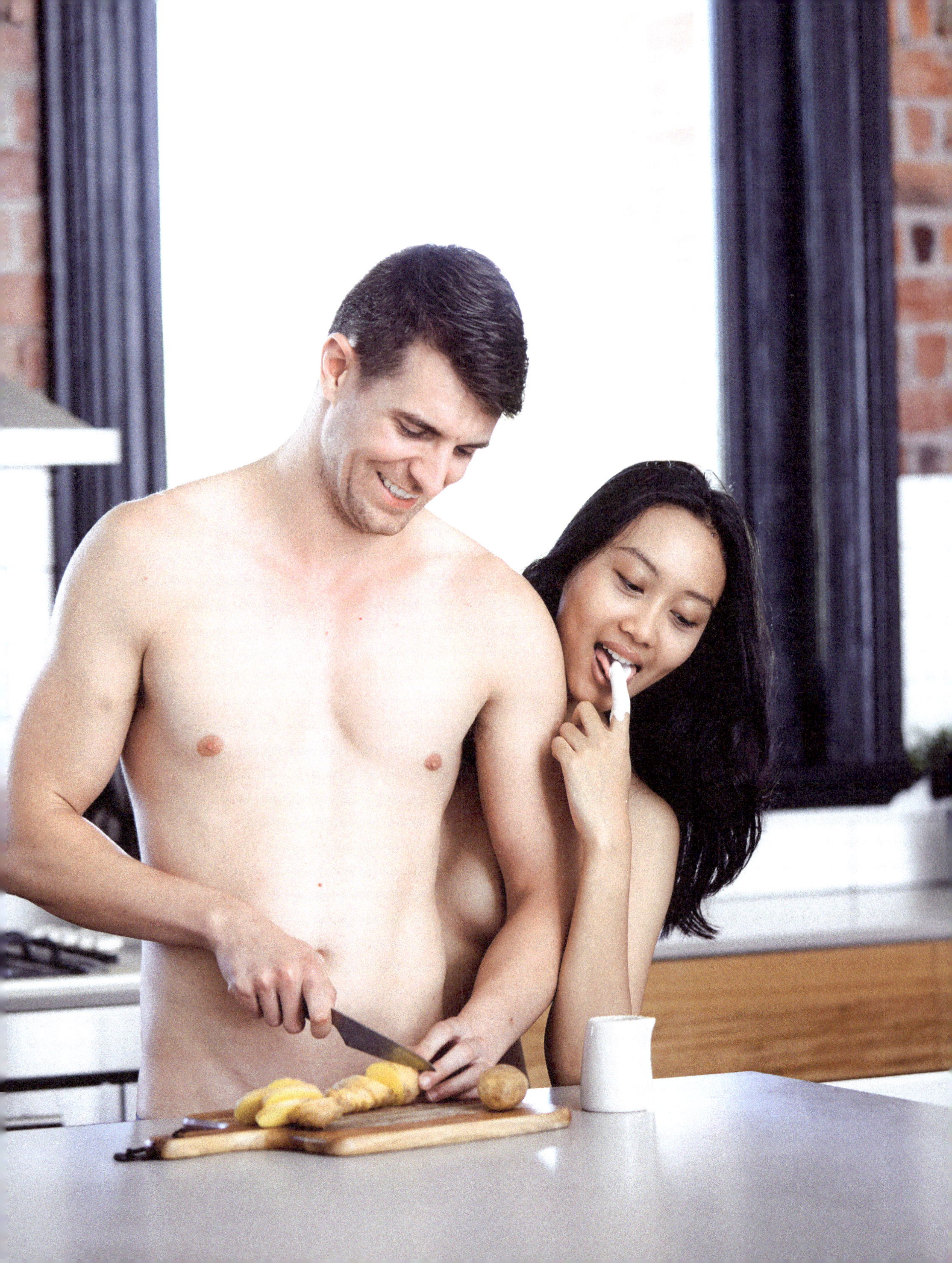

CREAMY MOUTHFUL

POTATO & FENNEL GRATIN

Fill your mouth up with a big creamy wad of gratin goodness. This is seriously delicious. Serve as is with a garden salad or as a side.

SERVES 6 AS A SIDE

3 Dutch cream potatoes
1 tbs olive oil, plus extra, to drizzle
½ red onion, sliced
½ fennel bulb, sliced, tossed in a little lemon juice to prevent browning
2 garlic cloves, finely chopped
200ml thickened cream
2 cups grated cheddar cheese

CRUMB

2 thick slices sourdough, cut into chunks
½ lemon, zested
½ garlic clove
½ cup grated cheddar cheese
1 thyme sprig, leaves picked
Handful parsley, roughly chopped
Salt and pepper

1. Preheat oven to 180C. Lightly grease a 2L-capacity baking dish.

2. Place potatoes in a pot of cold water and bring to a simmer over medium heat. Simmer for 10-15min or until potatoes are two-thirds of the way cooked, then drain and set aside to cool. Slice into 3mm-thick slices.

3. To make the crumb, place bread, lemon zest, garlic, salt and pepper in a food processor and process to a coarse crumb. Add cheese, thyme and parsley, and process again until combined.

4. Heat oil in a pan over medium heat. Add onion, fennel and garlic and cook for 4 minutes or until softened. Set aside.

5. Lightly coat the base of the baking dish with cream, then top with a layer of potato, salt and pepper, one-third of the cheese, half the fennel mixture and a generous drizzle of cream. Repeat this layering one more time then finish with a layer of potato, remaining cream, remaining cheese and finally the crumb mixture. Lightly drizzle extra oil over the crumb, and bake for 30 minutes or until crumb is golden and crunchy. Serve with a garden salad.

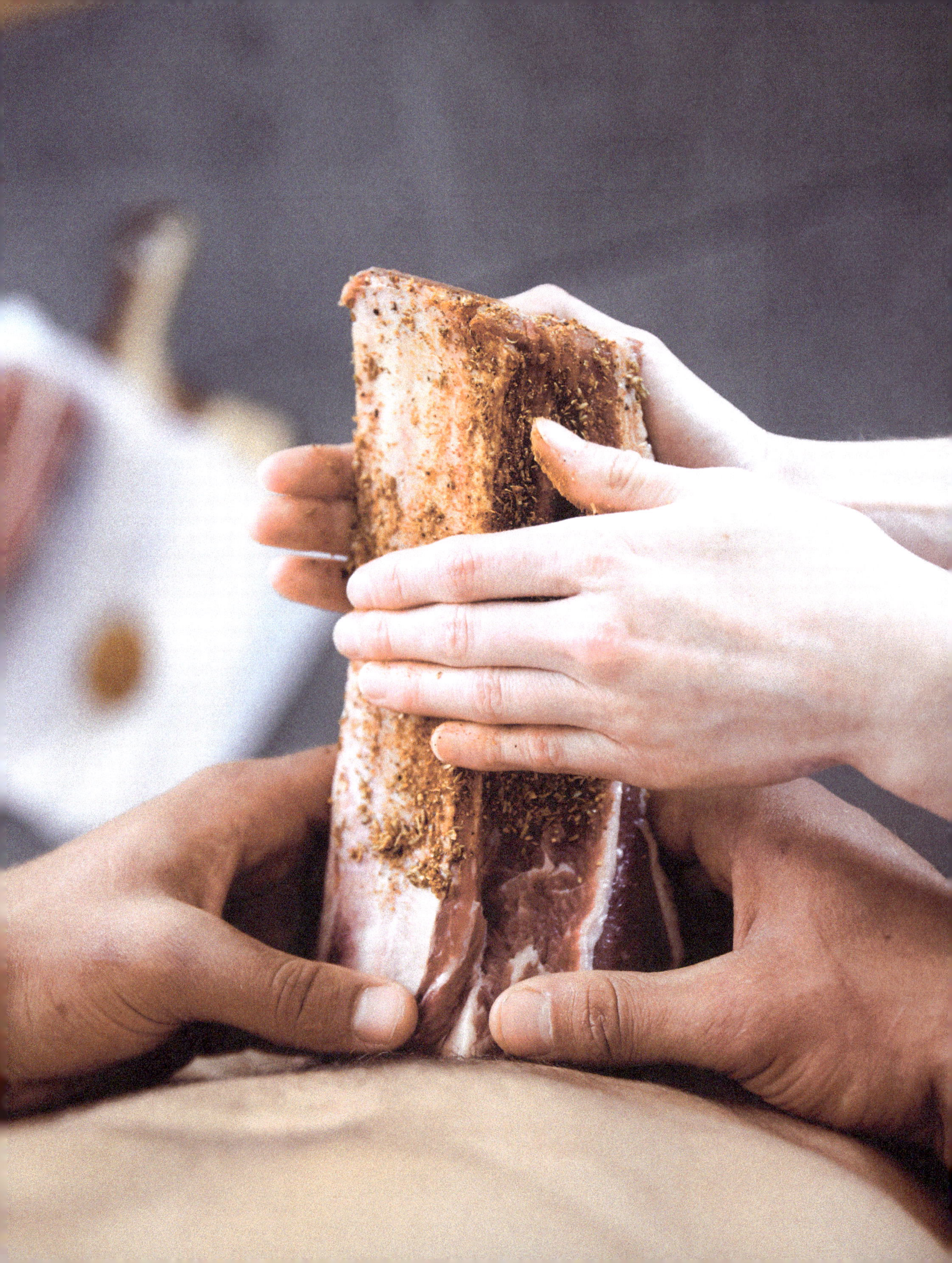

BIG BONE

SLOW-COOKED BEEF RIBS

You will be licking the bone up and down to ensure you don't miss out on any of this tender flavoursome meat.

SERVES 4

½ tsp black peppercorns
½ tsp fennel seeds
½ tsp cumin seeds
½ tsp coriander seeds
½ tsp salt
1 tsp smoked paprika
1 tsp chilli flakes
4 beef ribs, excess fat trimmed, if required
Lime wedges, to serve

BBQ SAUCE

¼ cup red wine
¼ cup brown sugar
¼ cup orange juice
2 tbs balsamic vinegar
2 tbs soy sauce
2 tbs ketjap manis
1 tsp smoked paprika
1 tsp sea salt

CUCUMBER VINAIGRETTE

2 tbs red wine vinegar
1 tsp caster sugar
½ tsp sea salt
1 long red chilli, finely chopped
Small handful fresh coriander, finely chopped
½ Lebanese cucumber, seeded, finely chopped

1. Preheat oven to 120C. Using a mortar and pestle, grind peppercorns, fennel, cumin and coriander to a rough powder, then mix through salt, paprika and chilli.

2. Rub spice mix all over ribs then wrap in baking paper followed by a tight layer of foil. Place ribs in a large heavy-based roasting pan and roast for 3 hours. Open up wrapping to expose ribs and roast for a further 1 hour or until meat easily pulls away from the bone and ribs have caramalised slightly. Remove from oven and set aside to cool for 15 minutes. Reserve roasting pan, but pour out excess juices.

3. Meanwhile, to make BBQ sauce, place all ingredients in a small pan over low heat. Cook, stirring, for 5 minutes or until sauce thickens.

4. Coat ribs all over with BBQ sauce and return to reserved roasting pan. Roast for a further 30 minutes, basting occasionally, until marinade is slightly caramelised.

5. Meanwhile, to make vinaigrette, combine vinegar, sugar and salt in a small bowl. Stir through remaining ingredients and set aside.

6. Serve ribs with cucumber vinaigrette and lime wedges.

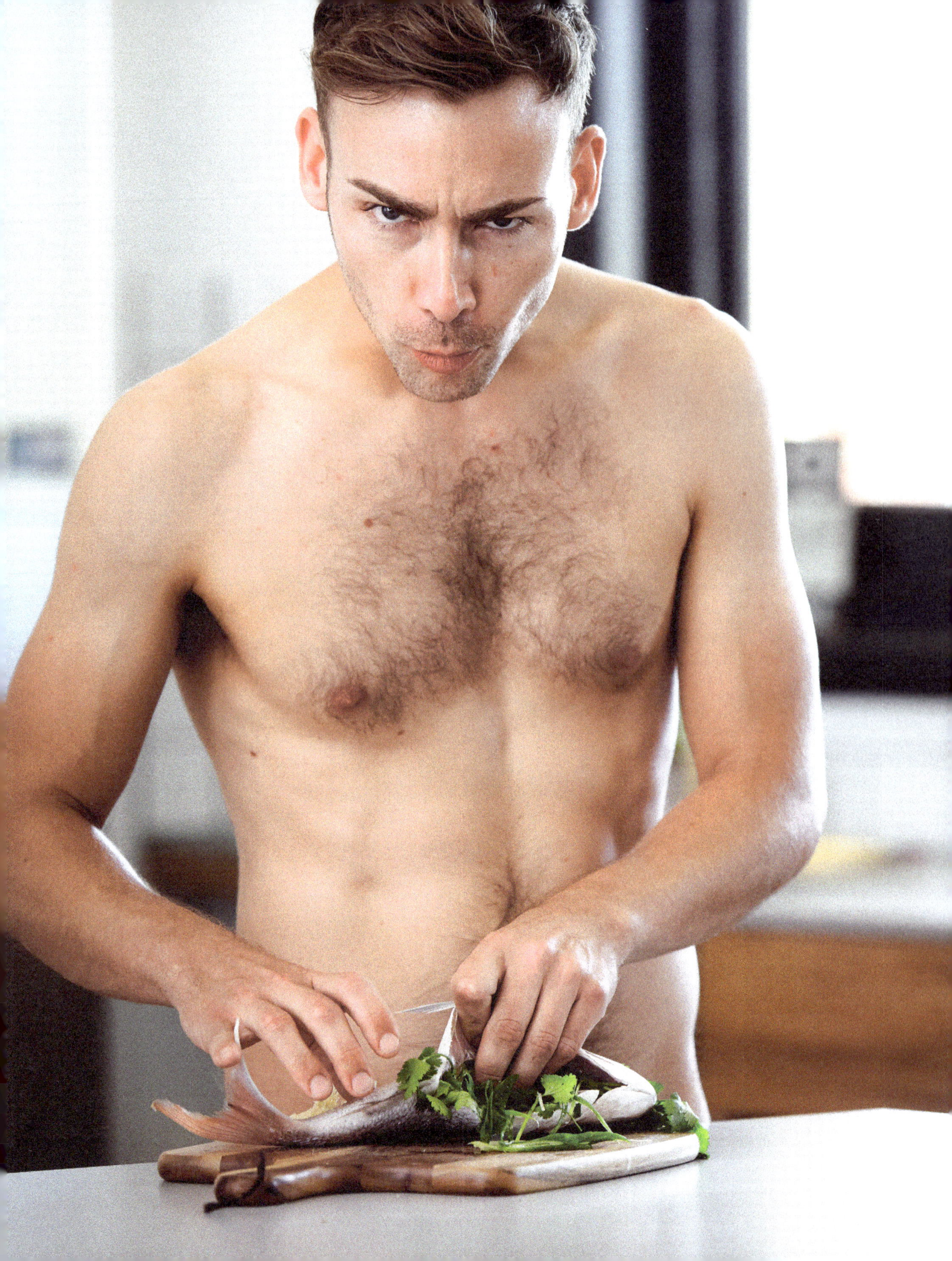

STUFF IT IN

INDIAN BAKED SNAPPER

A spicy light lunch or dinner. Be sure to help your loved one guide the goods deep into the cavity.

SERVES 2

2 x thumb-size pieces ginger, peeled
2 garlic cloves, peeled
½ thumb-size piece turmeric, peeled
2 coriander roots
1 tsp chilli flakes
½ tsp ground coriander seeds
½ tsp ground cumin seeds
1 tsp tamarind paste
1 tsp sea salt
1 tbs Greek yoghurt
2 tbs olive oil

1 whole snapper (600g-1kg)
Handful coriander, extra, washed, roots scraped
1 spring onion, sliced

SALAD
½ lime, juiced
½ tbs palm sugar, finely grated
2 tbs olive oil
1 cup cherry tomatoes, halved
Big handful coriander, roughly chopped
1 large shallot, thinly sliced
½ green chilli, thinly sliced (for a milder dish, substitute green capsicum)

1. To make marinade, using a mortar and pestle, bash 1 thumb-size piece of ginger, garlic, turmeric and coriander roots to a coarse paste, then stir in remaining spices, yoghurt and oil, and set aside.

2. Slice remaining ginger and stuff into fish cavity with extra coriander and spring onion. Lightly score flesh 5 times on each side, being careful not to cut all the way through the flesh. Rub marinade into both sides of the fish, place in an airtight container and marinate in the fridge for 30 minutes.

3. Preheat oven to 200C. Place marinated fish onto an oven tray lined with baking paper and roast for 20-25 minutes, or until just cooked. Cooking time will depend on size of fish.

4. Meanwhile, to make salad dressing, in a small bowl dissolve palm sugar and a pinch of salt in lime juice, then stir in oil. Place remaining salad ingredients in a bowl and toss with dressing.

5. Serve baked snapper with salad.

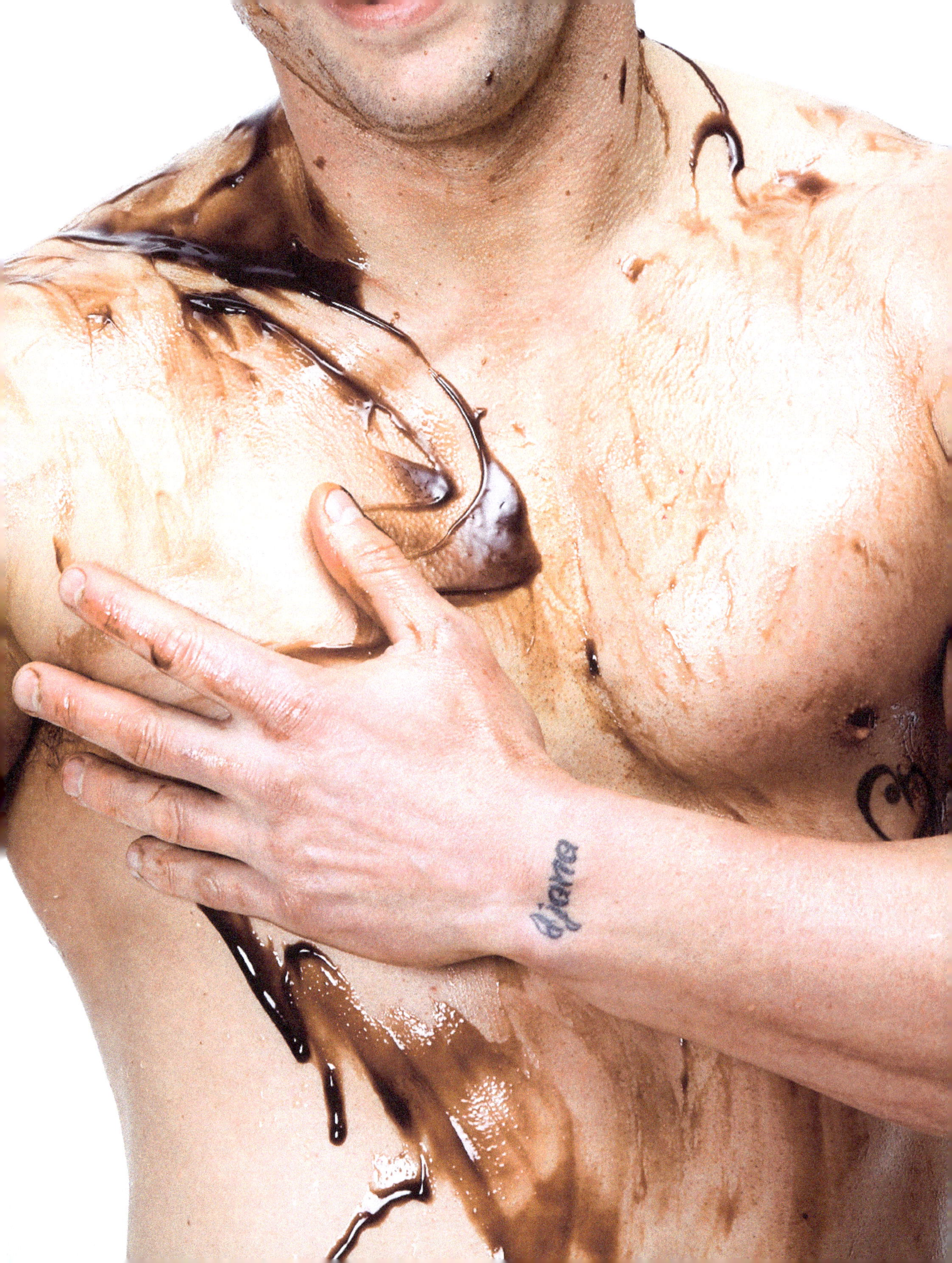

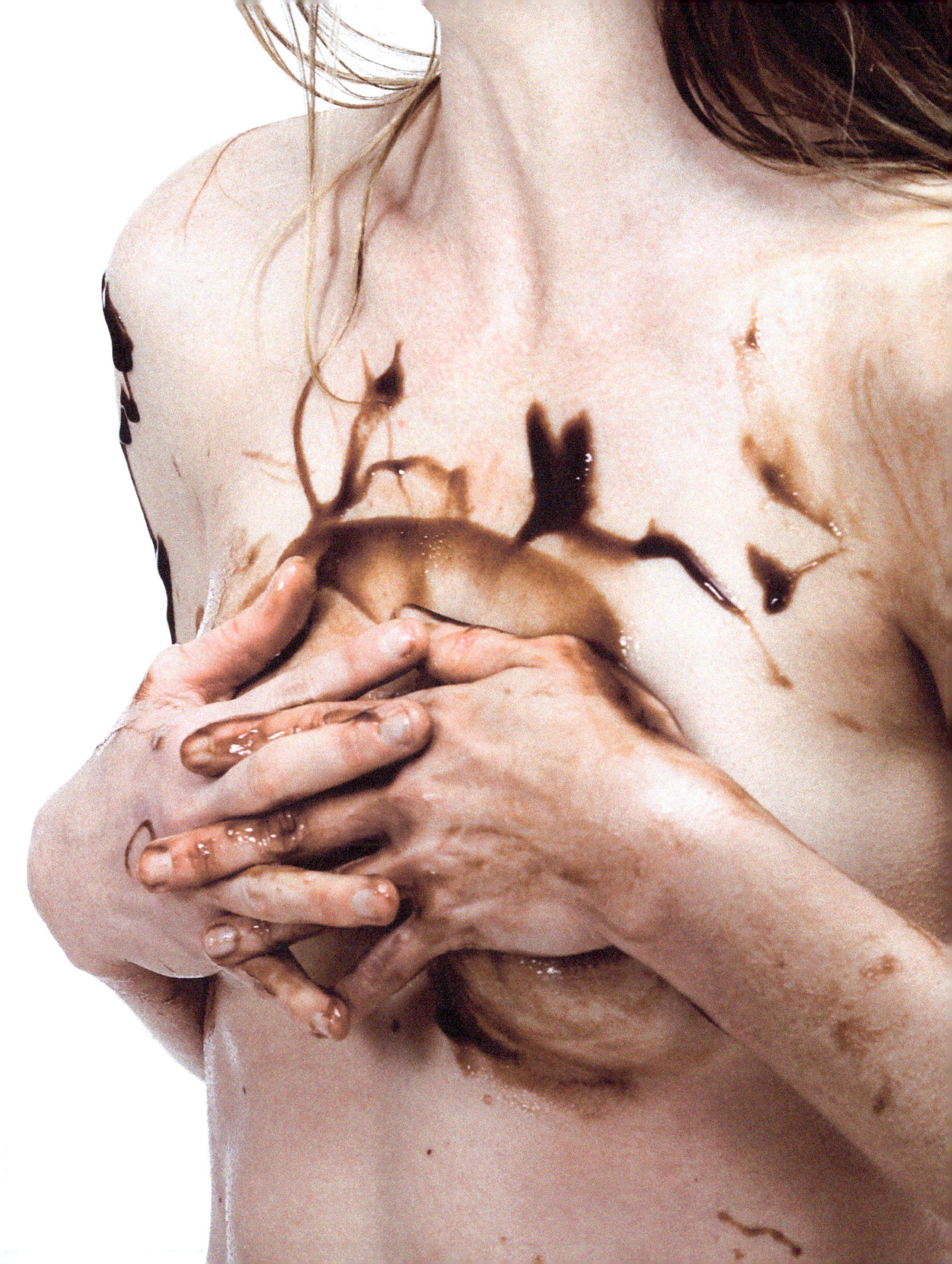

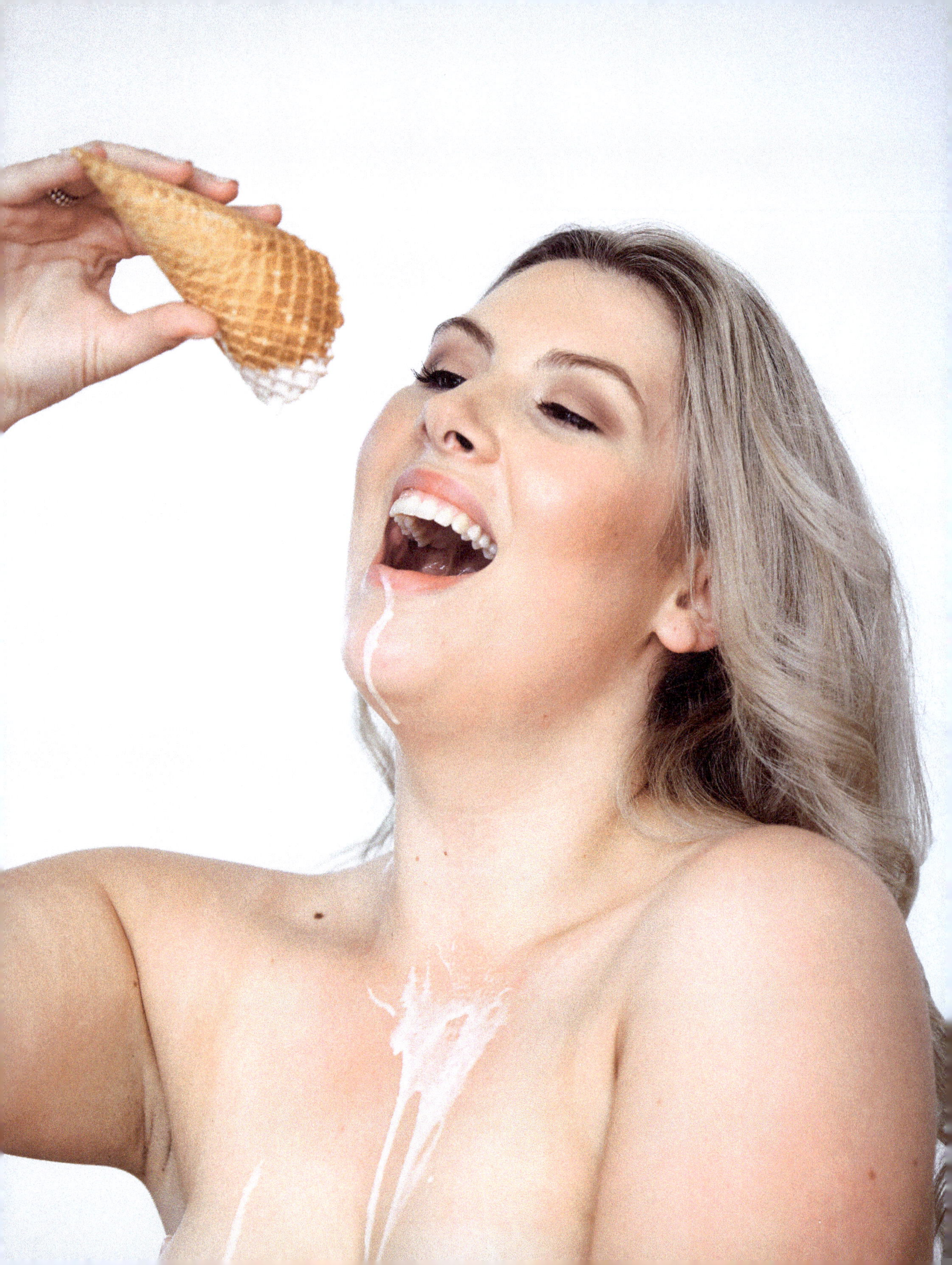

MONEY SHOT

SEMIFREDDO

MAKES 2L

3 eggs
2 egg yolks, extra
1 cup caster sugar
2 tsp vanilla bean extract
600ml cream
3 x 50g chocolate honeycomb bars, crushed, to serve

Basically an easy no churn homemade ice-cream recipe – which may end up all over your face after a good licking. You can add whatever you like to the base – fresh berries, rum-soaked raisins and nuts all work well.

1. Place eggs, extra yolks, sugar and vanilla in a heatproof bowl over a pot of simmering water on a very low heat. Using an electric mixer, beat for 8 minutes or until thick and luscious and warm to touch (do not let the bowl get too hot). Set aside to cool slightly.

2. Whisk cream until stiff peaks form. Gently fold through egg mix in 2 batches until well combined then fold through two of the crushed honeycomb bars. Transfer mixture to an airtight container and freeze for 4-6 hours or until set. Serve topped with crushed honeycomb.

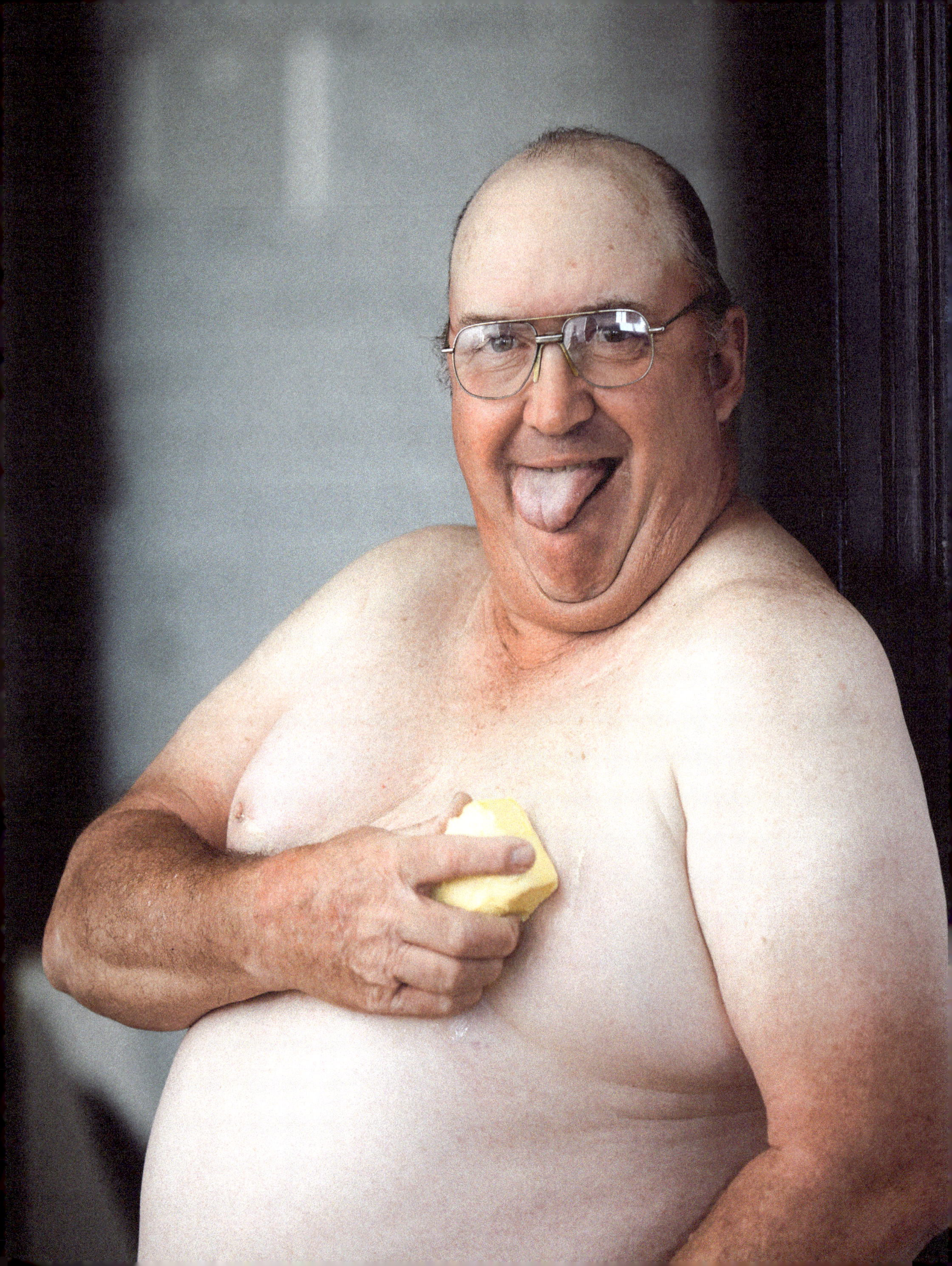

BUTTER ME UP
BREAD AND BUTTER PUDDING

Slide a spoon into this old school buttery slab of creamy goodness and enjoy

SERVES 6-8

1 cup sultanas
¼ cup brandy
5 eggs
300ml thickened cream
500ml full cream milk
¼ cup caster sugar
2 tsp vanilla bean paste
1 tsp ground cinnamon
1 tsp ground cardamom
10 thin slices of 2-day-old white bread
100g unsalted butter, softened
2 tbs demerara sugar
Crème fraîche or ice-cream, to serve

1. Combine sultanas and brandy in a small heatproof bowl and microwave for 1 minute, then stir, and set aside.

2. In a large jug whisk together eggs, cream, milk, caster sugar, vanilla, cinnamon and cardamom.

3. Butter both sides of bread, then slice in half.

4. Lightly grease a 2L-capacity baking dish, then layer pudding with one-third of sultana mixture, half the bread slices, another third of the sultana mixture and remaining bread. Top with remaining sultanas.

5. Pour cream mixture over the top and gently press down sultanas and bread so it is flat. Cover and set aside for 30 minutes.

6. Meanwhile, preheat oven to 180C. Scatter demerara sugar over pudding and bake for 30 minutes or until just set. Remove from oven and then place under grill on high heat for 5 minutes or until golden brown. Serve pudding with crème fraîche or ice-cream.

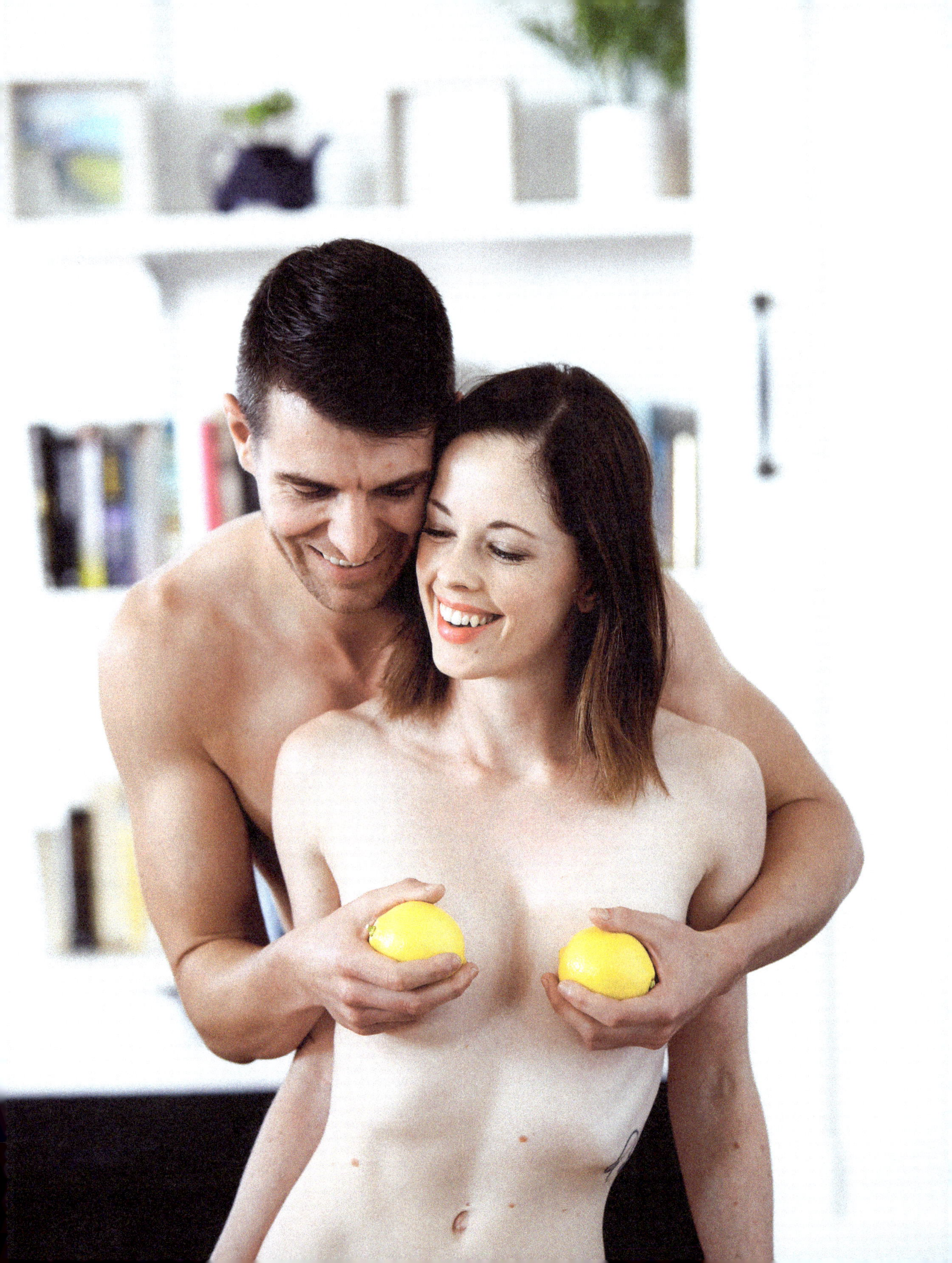

BIG TART

LEMON TART

This recipe is quite tart but very enjoyable, especially when shared with friends. If you're not up for making the pastry from scratch, simply use pre-made frozen shortcrust pastry, instead.

SERVES 6-8

300ml thickened cream

2 eggs

4 egg yolks, extra

½ cup caster sugar

1 lemon, zested

150ml lemon juice

200ml double cream

1 tsp vanilla bean paste

Icing sugar and fresh berries, to serve

SHORTCRUST PASTRY

1 ½ cups plain flour

125g chilled unsalted butter, chopped

½ cup caster sugar

3 extra-large egg yolks

1. To make shortcrust pastry, place flour, butter, sugar and a pinch of salt in a food processor and quickly process until mixture resembles fine crumbs. With the motor running, add egg yolks and process until combined. Add 1 tbs cold water and process until dough just comes together. Turn dough out onto a lightly floured work surface and gently bring together to form a disc. Wrap in plastic wrap and refrigerate for 30 minutes.

2. Using a rolling pin, roll pastry out between 2 sheets of non-stick baking paper to 3-5mm thick. Line a lightly greased 25cm loose-bottomed tart tin with pastry. Trim edges and prick base with a fork. Refrigerate for 30 minutes.

3. Meanwhile, preheat oven to 180C. Line chilled pastry case with non-stick baking paper and fill with baking weights or uncooked rice. Bake for 15 minutes, then remove paper and weights and return to oven for a further 10-15 minutes, or until pastry is light golden. Remove and set aside. Reduce oven to 140C.

4. To make lemon filling, place cream, eggs, extra yolks, sugar, lemon zest and juice in a bowl and whisk to combine. Pour filling into tart shell.

5. Bake for 30-40 minutes or until just set – the filling should have a wobble to it but not look runny. Remove from oven and set aside to cool at room temperature before refrigerating until completely set.

6. Meanwhile, in a small bowl, combine double cream and vanilla, and set aside in the fridge.

7. To serve, cut tart into portions, dust with icing sugar and accompany with fresh berries and vanilla cream.

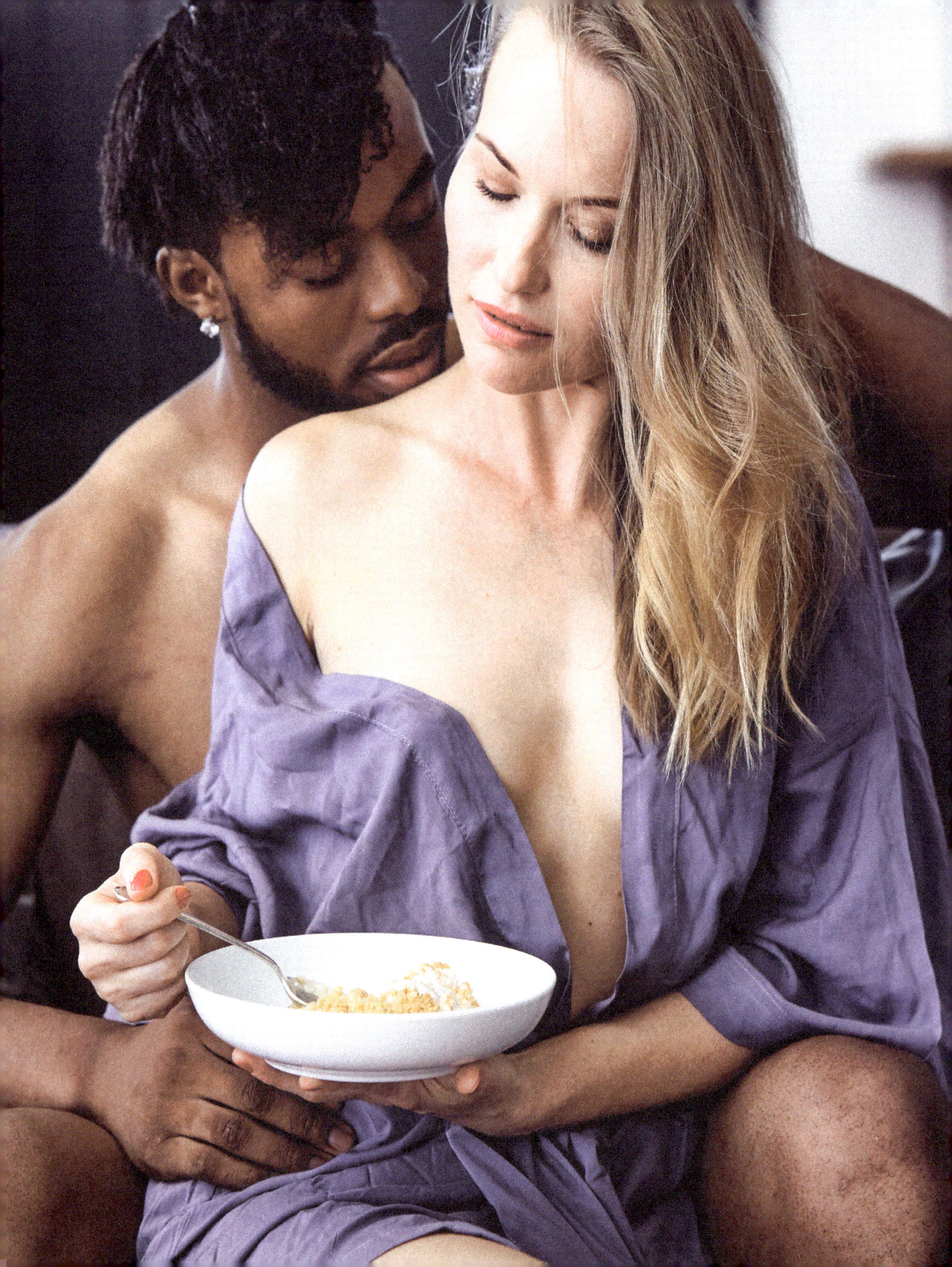

MAKE ME CRUMBLE

APPLE CRUMBLE

A classic heartwarming dessert that will leave your loved one quivering with delight.

SERVES 6-8

6 granny smith apples, peeled, cored, cut into 2cm pieces
1 cup caster sugar
½ lemon, juiced
1 ½ tsp ground cinnamon
1 tsp vanilla bean extract
1 cup plain flour
1 cup rolled oats
½ cup almond meal
200g unsalted butter, melted
Vanilla ice-cream or double cream, to serve

1. Preheat oven to 180C. Place apple, 1/2 cup sugar, lemon juice, 1/2 tsp cinnamon and vanilla in a large pot over medium heat and cook, stirring occasionally, for 5 minutes or until sugar has dissolved and apple has softened a little.

2. To make crumble topping, combine flour, remaining 1/2 cup sugar, 1 tsp cinnamon, oats, almond meal and butter in a large bowl.

3. Transfer apple mixture to a 1.5L-capacity ovenproof dish, then spoon over crumble mixture.

4. Bake for 40–45 minutes, or until crumble is golden and apples are soft. Serve with vanilla ice-cream or double cream.

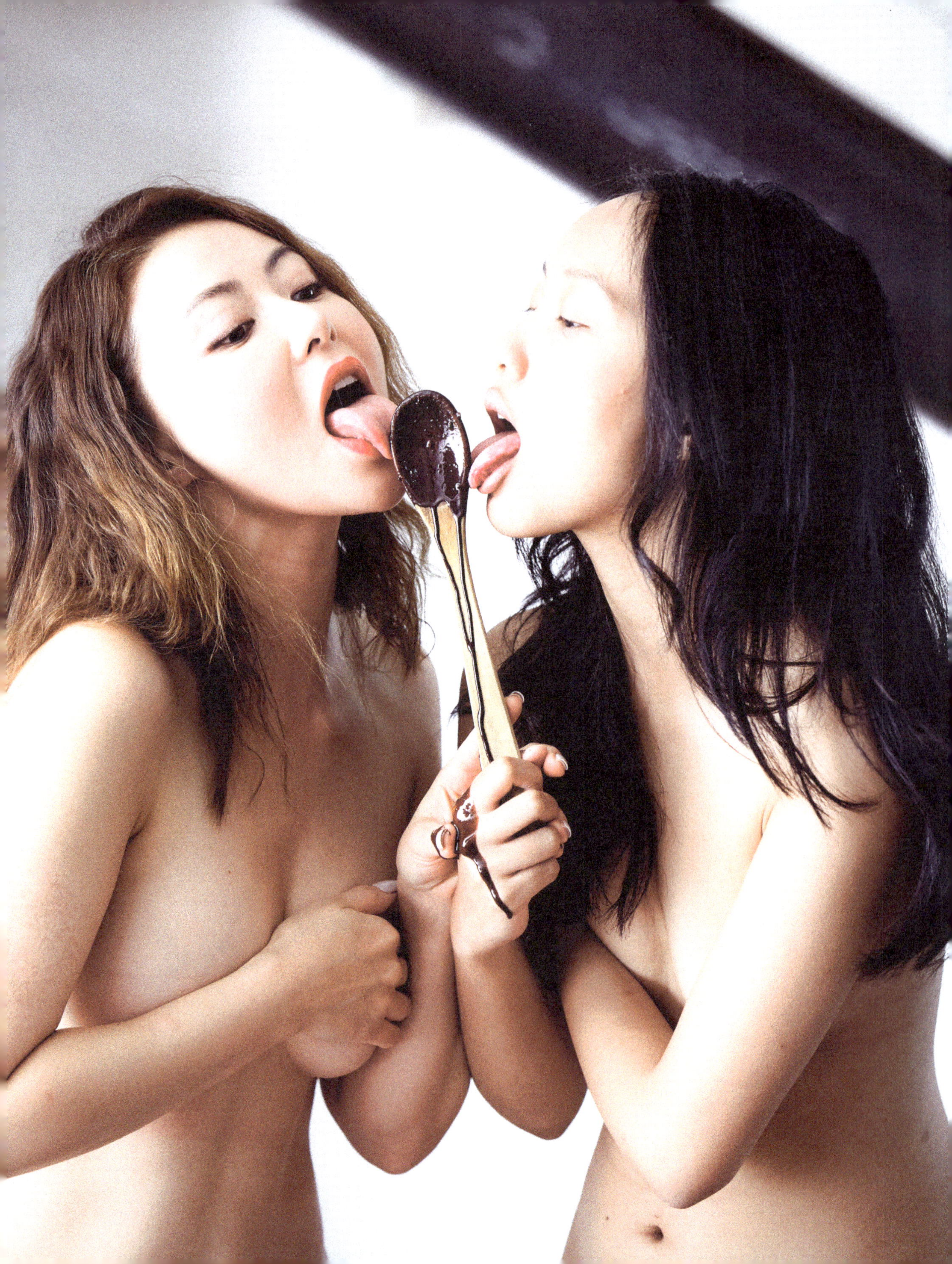

GETTING SAUCY

SELF-SAUCING CHOCOLATE PUDDING

Is there anything sexier than oozy warm chocolate? Licking the spoon is compulsory.

SERVES 6-8

1 cup self-raising flour
⅓ cup caster sugar
⅓ cup cocoa powder
½ cup milk
40g butter, melted
1 free-range egg, whisked
½ tsp vanilla bean extract
60g dark cooking chocolate, roughly chopped
⅓ cup brown sugar
Double cream or ice-cream to serve

1. Preheat oven to 180C. Grease a 1L-capacity baking dish. Sift flour, sugar and 2 tbs cocoa into a mixing bowl, then add milk, butter, egg and vanilla and stir until combined. Pour into the baking dish and push dark chocolate pieces into the mix.

2. Combine sugar, remaining 2 tbs cocoa and 1 cup boiling water in a jug and mix well until sugar is dissolved. Slowly pour sauce mixture over pudding.

3. Bake for 20–25 minutes or until firm to touch. Serve warm with double cream or ice-cream.

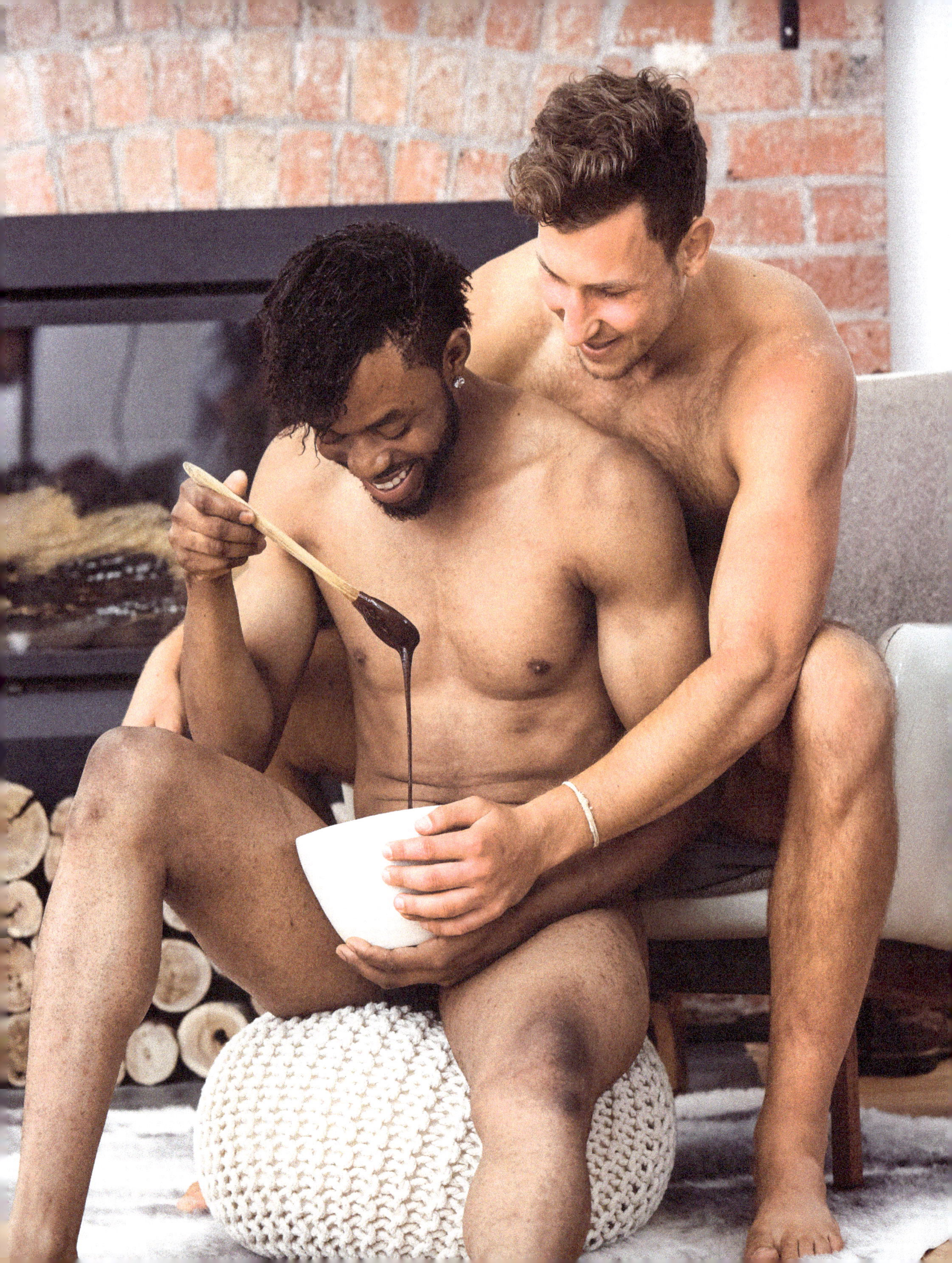

SEXUAL CHOCOLATE

SALTED CARAMEL CHOCOLATE BROWNIES

Do your best Ghost impersonation by lending a helping hand. This recipe makes more fudge than you'll need for the brownies, so you'll have extra on hand to serve separately, or just when you're in need of a cheeky afternoon delight.

MAKES 6 BROWNIES

200g dark cooking chocolate, chopped

250g butter, chopped

1 ½ cups brown sugar

4 eggs

½ cup cocoa powder, sifted

1 ¼ cups of plain flour, sifted

¼ tsp baking powder

Double cream and chopped walnuts, to serve

CARAMEL FUDGE

1 x 397g can condensed milk

125g unsalted butter, chopped

⅓ cup brown sugar

¾ cup golden syrup

1 tsp vanilla bean extract

180g white cooking chocolate, roughly chopped

1 tsp sea salt

1. To make caramel fudge, line a 20cm square cake tin with baking paper. Place condensed milk, butter, sugar, golden syrup and vanilla in a pan over medium heat, and cook, stirring, for 5 minutes or until sugar has melted.

2. Bring mixture to a gentle boil and stir constantly for 10 minutes or until mixture darkens slightly; don't let mixture get too dark. Remove from heat, add white chocolate and salt and stir until chocolate has melted.

3. Pour fudge mixture into prepared tin. Leave to cool at room temperature for 30 minutes, then refrigerate for a further 3-4 hours to set.

4. Chop fudge into 2cm square pieces and set aside. Store extra fudge in an airtight container in the fridge.

5. To make brownies, preheat oven to 160C. Line a 20cm cake tin with baking paper. Place chocolate and butter in a saucepan over low heat and cook, stirring, until chocolate has melted. Remove from heat and set aside to cool slightly.

6. Place remaining ingredients in a bowl, then add chocolate mixture and stir until combined. Pour brownie mixture into prepared tin. Press 6 fudge squares into the mix. Bake for 50 minutes or until crumbs cling to a skewer inserted in the middle. Set aside to cool in the tin for 15 minutes, then transfer to a wire rack to cool for a further 15 minutes.

7. To serve, slice brownie into 6 squares and top with a dollop of double cream and chopped walnuts.

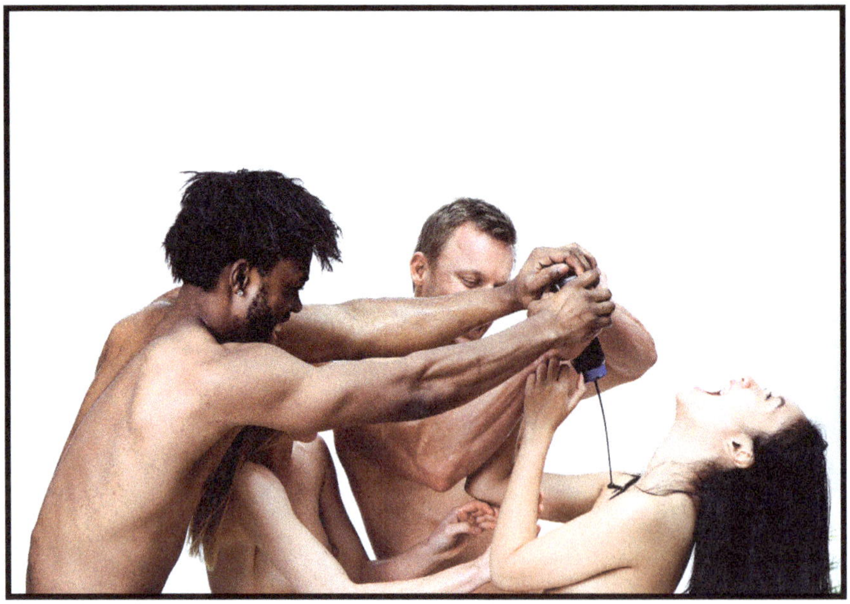

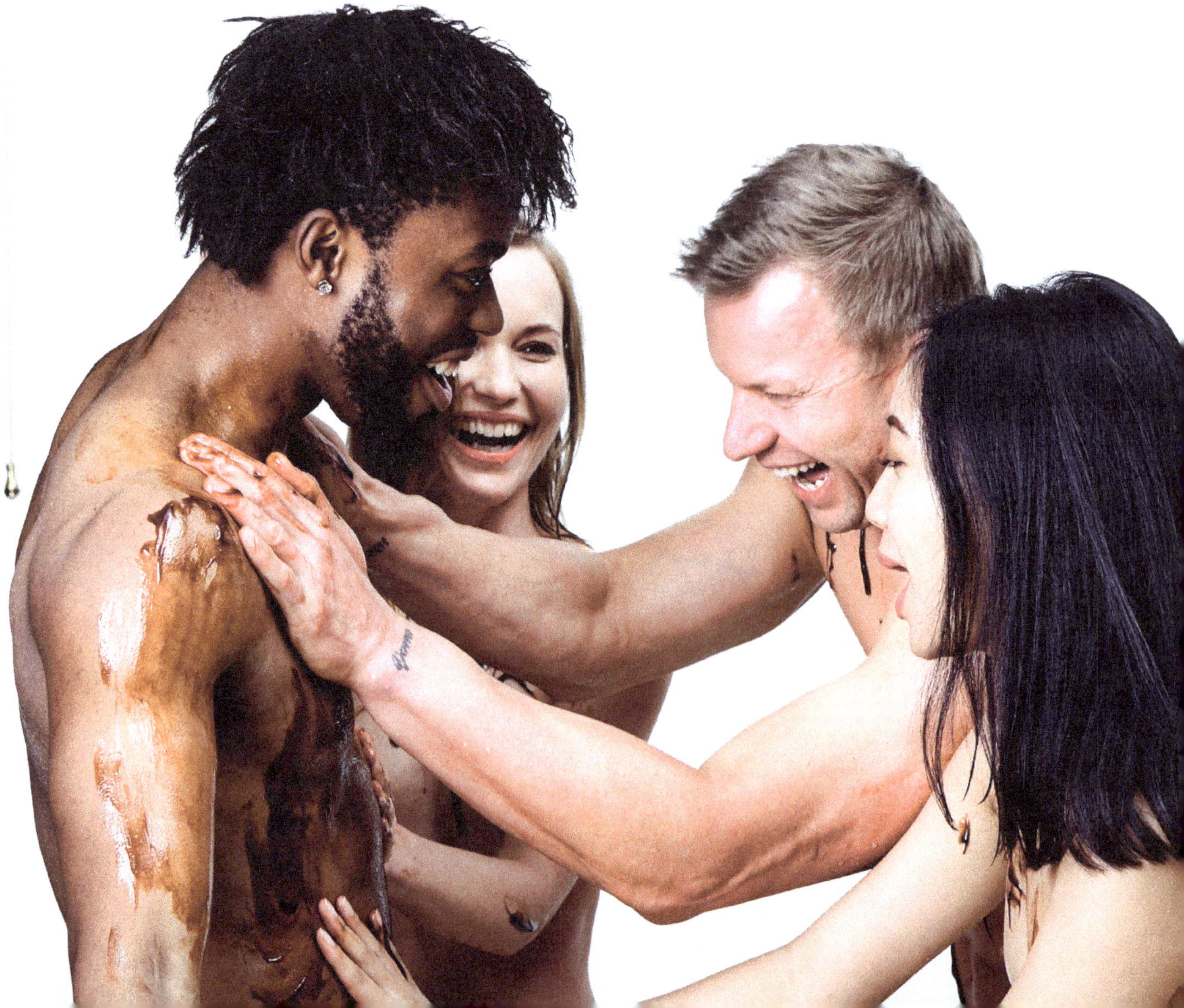

ACKNOWLEDGEMENTS

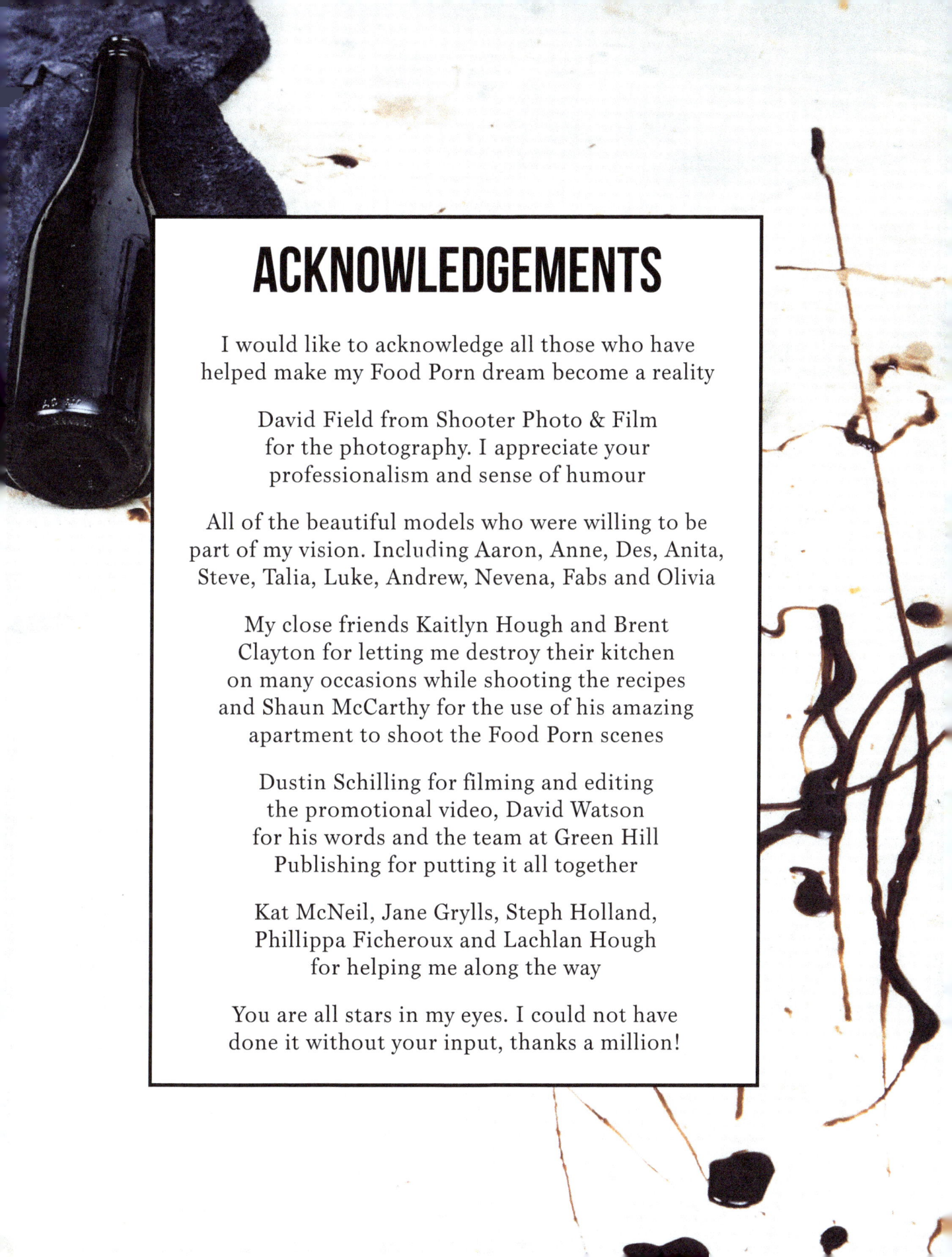

I would like to acknowledge all those who have helped make my Food Porn dream become a reality

David Field from Shooter Photo & Film for the photography. I appreciate your professionalism and sense of humour

All of the beautiful models who were willing to be part of my vision. Including Aaron, Anne, Des, Anita, Steve, Talia, Luke, Andrew, Nevena, Fabs and Olivia

My close friends Kaitlyn Hough and Brent Clayton for letting me destroy their kitchen on many occasions while shooting the recipes and Shaun McCarthy for the use of his amazing apartment to shoot the Food Porn scenes

Dustin Schilling for filming and editing the promotional video, David Watson for his words and the team at Green Hill Publishing for putting it all together

Kat McNeil, Jane Grylls, Steph Holland, Phillippa Ficheroux and Lachlan Hough for helping me along the way

You are all stars in my eyes. I could not have done it without your input, thanks a million!

First published in 2017

© Beau Cook

The moral rights of the author have been asserted.

All rights reserved. Except as permitted under the Australian Copyright Act 1968 (for example, a fair dealing for the purposes of study, research, criticism or review), no part of this book may be reproduced, stored in a retrieval system, communicated or transmitted in any form or by any means without prior written permission.

All inquiries should be made to the author.

National Library of Australia Cataloguing-in-Publication entry:

Creator:	Cook, Beau, author.
Title:	Beau Cook's Food Porn
ISBN:	978-0-6481379-8-6 (paperback)

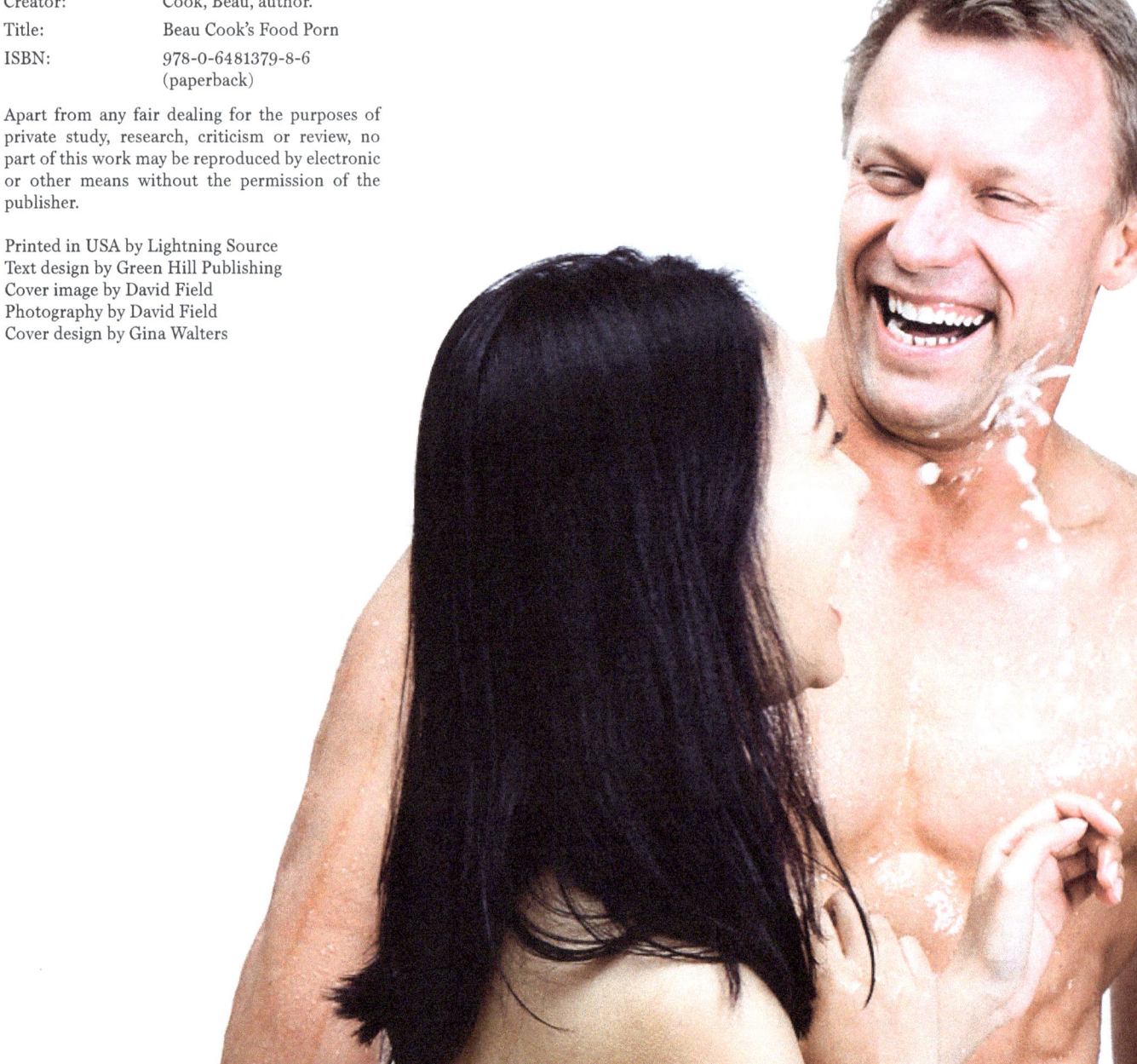

Apart from any fair dealing for the purposes of private study, research, criticism or review, no part of this work may be reproduced by electronic or other means without the permission of the publisher.

Printed in USA by Lightning Source
Text design by Green Hill Publishing
Cover image by David Field
Photography by David Field
Cover design by Gina Walters

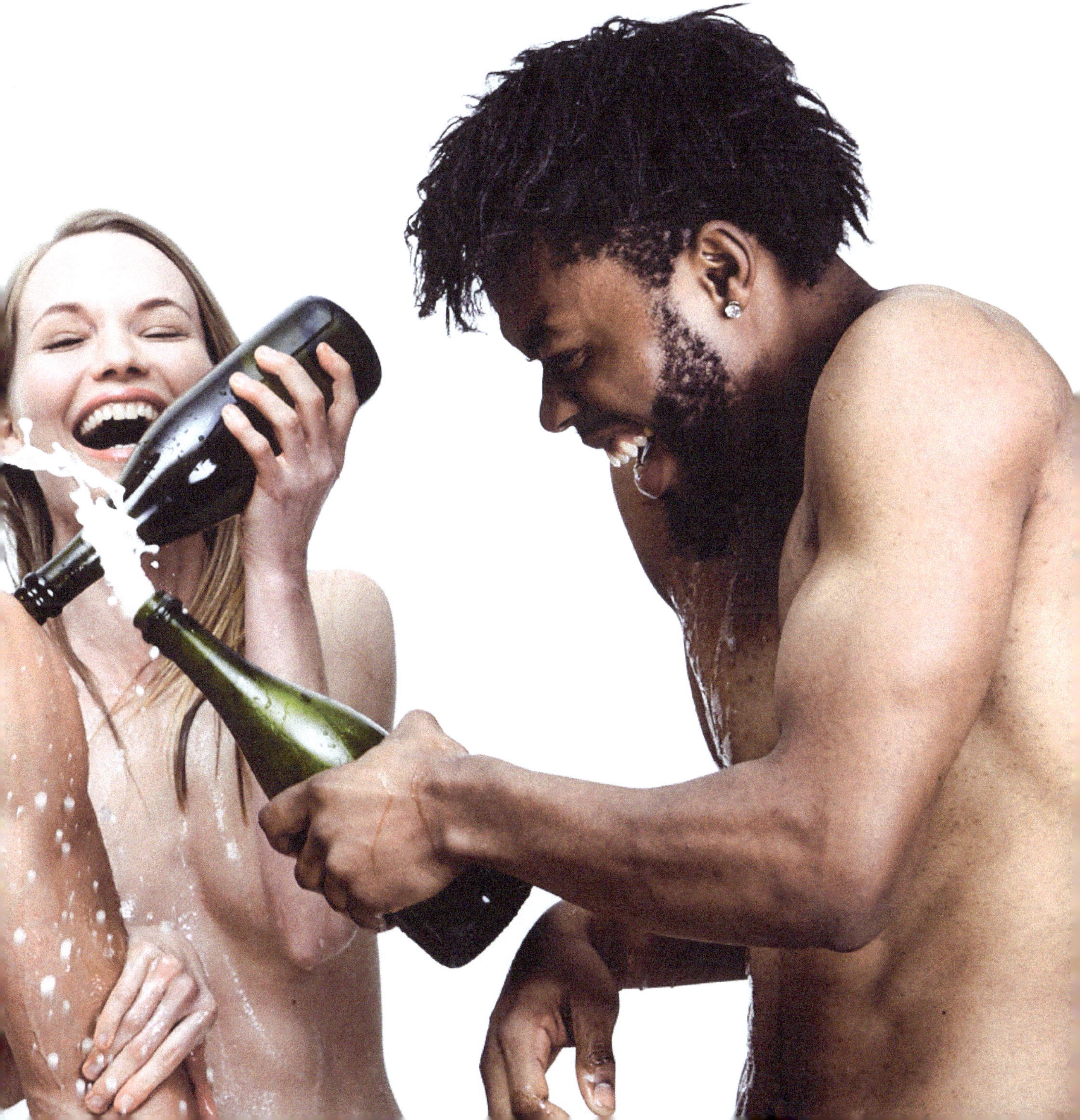

BEAU COOK'S FOOD PORN

WWW.BEAUCOOKSFOODPORN.COM

Lightning Source UK Ltd.
Milton Keynes UK
UKHW050235021118
331601UK00003B/37/P